LIVING THE
EXCHANGE

A DISCIPLE'S BIBLE STUDY

JEFF MUSGRAVE

journey**forth**®

Greenville, South Carolina

Cover istockphoto/phakimata

All Scripture is quoted from the Authorized King James Version.

Living the Exchange
Jeff Musgrave

Cover Design and Page Layout by Peter Crane
© 2010 by BJU Press
Greenville, South Carolina 29614
JourneyForth Books is a division of BJU Press

ISBN 978-1-60682-156-5

15   14   13   12   11   10   9   8   7   6   5   4

This book is dedicated to my partner, best friend, and amazing wife, Anna.
It is part of the fruit produced in the valleys of our life,
and she has faithfully walked beside me every step of the way.
Thank you, sweetheart. The truths from God's Word found in this book
were taught to us by the blessed Holy Spirit. He is the teacher;
the Bible is His textbook; the circumstances
of our life are His classroom; and our precious Lord Jesus is His Subject!

CONTENTS

Foreword vii

Acknowledgments ix

How to Use This Bible Study x

Enrollment Form xi

Living the Exchange Commitment xii

1 My New Inheritance 1
   Understanding What I Inherited When I Received Christ

2 My Bible 11
   Understanding the Foundational Nature of the Word of God

3 My Baptism and Church Membership 20
   Understanding Public Identification with Christ and Joining a Bible-believing Church

4 The Futility of My Self 29
   Understanding the Inability of the Flesh to Please God

5 The Fullness of My Savior 38
   Understanding the Promise of Christ's Life in Me

6 The Fountain of My Surrender 46
   Appropriating the Power of God in My Life

7 The Filling of My Spirit 58
   Experiencing the Realities of God's Grace in My Life

8 The Holy Spirit and My Changing Life 68
   How to Live as a Spirit-filled Christian in a Sinful World

9 The Holy Spirit and My Prayer Life 78
   How to Access God's Throne of Grace

10 The Holy Spirit and My Home Life 90
   How to Live as a Spirit-filled Member of My Family

11 The Holy Spirit and My Financial Life 103
   How to Adopt God's Attitude Toward My Money

12 The Fruitfulness of My Service 115
   Fulfilling the Purpose of the Spirit-filled Life—Service for the King

FOREWORD

There is nothing more majestic than the sight of a mature eagle soaring through a cloudless sky. The Bible uses this picture to describe a mature Christian who has learned to live in the strength that the Lord supplies.

> *Isaiah 40:31—But they that wait upon the Lord shall renew their strength; they shall mount up with wings as eagles; they shall run, and not be weary; and they shall walk, and not faint.*

The words in this verse were carefully chosen by God to communicate a wonderful message.

- Wait upon—long for, tarry with, bind to

- Renew—come on anew, substitute or change for better

- Weary—cause to become toilsome

When a Christian learns how to live out of the resources God gave him at salvation, he is constantly supplied with new energy from God.

> *Lamentations 3:22–23—It is of the Lord's mercies that we are not consumed, because his compassions fail not. They are new every morning: great is [Your] faithfulness.*

These energies from God are real and should be the norm for the Christian. The key is to live in connection to Him, Who is the source. When our relationship with God is intimate and vibrant, the Bible says we can expect renewed strength, or revival, every day. The excitement of living with Him doesn't need to grow old and wearisome. Don't be content with a duty-filled life of religion. As you study these lessons, ask God to show you the reality of a passion-filled relationship of renewal with God.

Eaglets are born with instincts to fly, but they must acquire the skills to do so. In a similar way a new Christian has an appetite for an intimate relationship with God but not the acquired skills. This Bible study is designed to help you begin learning to live with God.

Eagle parents cannot tell juveniles how to hunt. They have to learn by watching the parents and by practicing. The process is an interesting one. Fledglings (eaglets with the feathers necessary for flight) are still fed in the nest for several weeks. During that time the eaglets learn to spread their wings, and even allow the wind to pick them up, but often they must be coaxed from the nest by hunger. The parent birds will stop feeding the fledgling but will be prepared to do so immediately upon landing from his first flight. Eagles build their nests in the heights of trees and cliffs. About half of young eagles survive their first year. This is due to the trial and error method of developing the basic skills of flying and hunting.

God made some unusual promises to the infant nation of Israel that also apply to growing Christians.

> *Exodus 19:4—[You] have seen what I did unto the Egyptians, and how I bare you on eagles' wings, and brought you unto myself.*

> *Deuteronomy 32:10–12—He found him [Israel] in a desert land, and in the waste howling wilderness; he led him about, he instructed him, he kept him as the apple of his eye. As an eagle stirs up her nest, flutters over her young, spreads abroad her wings, takes them, bears them on her wings: so the Lord alone did lead him.*

God Himself wants to be your instructor. He wants the very learning process to be an intimate experience with Him. It is a dangerous journey. Many new Christians never reach maturity because of the pitfalls along the way, but you have an advantage over eaglets in that God is personally willing to carry you on His wings, and even to protect you under His wings as a mother eagle does her young.

> *Psalms 36:7—How excellent is your loving kindness, O God! Therefore the children of men put their trust under the shadow of thy wings.*

Your success or failure is based on your willingness to stay close to Him. Apply yourself to the study of His Word in this Bible study. Ask Him to teach you as you read. He is the living God and wants to have a real, vibrant relationship with you.

ACKNOWLEDGMENTS

Our pastors during the early years of our ministry, Drs. John Vaughn and Ed Nelson, faithfully taught and modeled the truths found in this book to us. Years ago these truths were forcefully driven from my head to my heart through some very painful circumstances. I was seeking comfort and counsel from Dr. Bob Wood when he told me, "Don't worry about it, Jeff. Though there are great vistas from the mountaintops, all of the best fruit is grown in the valleys."

At the time I responded, "There's no fruit down here. It just stinks."

Dr. Wood was right and the work God has done in my heart was worth the hurt of the valley. My dear wife, Anna, has agonized over the words of this book as much as I have. Our good friend Mary Ellen Norwood was less than a year old in the Lord when she loaned us her timeshare to allow us time to finish the book while we were still very busy in the pastorate. She not only spent many hours helping us with the wording and editing, but she tried on the truths and reminded us again that they work. It was through her that we met Michael and Renee, who introduced us to Jonathan and Monica, all of whom are now on their way to heaven and learning to "live the exchange." Our work would never have happened without the support and encouragement of our church family at Highlands Baptist. Our ministry partner Justine Prahl has poured herself into the pages through many hours of loving labor. Les Heinze, Aaron Merrick, Jeff Redlin, Kevin Schaal, Brad Smith, and Dave Shumate have all made this a better book through their careful reading and helpful comments. May the Lord use the combined efforts of these and many others not mentioned to impact many for Spirit-empowered living and ministry.

HOW TO USE THIS BIBLE STUDY

During the next twelve weeks you will learn many exciting truths from God's Word! Plan to do only one lesson each week so that you can concentrate on it and carefully complete it. Each lesson includes Bible verses to read, questions to answer, a verse to memorize, and a practical assignment to complete. Follow the simple guidelines below to get the most out of each lesson.

LOOK

Read each verse thoughtfully. All the Scriptures in this Bible study are taken from the King James Version of the Bible. Some of the words from the KJV are used differently in today's English and are followed by modern words in brackets [ ]. Some pronouns and verb endings have also been modernized. ***Note***: The answer is highlighted in bold print in each verse.

LIST

Answer all the questions thoroughly based on the information given in the Bible verse. If you do not understand a question, leave it blank and ask your Bible study leader about it at your next meeting. Make note of any other questions you may have in the margin.

LEARN

Understand what God is teaching you from the Bible and how it applies directly to you. Memorize the verse at the end of each lesson. The word *disciple* originates from the Latin word *discipulus*, "learner." Be a good learner!

LOVE

This Bible study is about learning to live with God. Your relationship with Him is born out of His love for you and grows as you learn to love Him in return. "We love him, because he first loved us" (1 John 4:19).

LIVE

Obey what God's Word tells you to do. This is the way to be happy and grow as a Christian. Christ said, "If [you] love me, keep my commandments" (John 14:15).

When you complete the course, you will be presented a certificate. Determine now that you will finish. Remember, your Bible study leader is your friend and is ready to help you in any way possible. Record your leader's name and phone number below.

Bible study leader: _____ Phone: _____

ENROLLMENT FORM

PERSONAL INFORMATION

Name _____ Birth date ____ / ____ / _____

Phone_____ Email _____

Address _____ Apt. # _____

City _____ State _____ Zip _____

CHURCH BACKGROUND INFORMATION

Church attendance per month (circle): 0 1 2 3 4 5 6 7 8 9 10+

Church attended in childhood _____

How often do you read the Bible (circle)? Never Occasionally Regularly

How were you introduced to this church? _____

Do you currently attend a Sunday school class? _____

FAMILY INFORMATION

Marital status (circle):   Single   Married   Separated   Divorced   Widowed

List the names of your spouse and any children or other relatives living with you.

Name	Relation	Birthdate
_____	_____	____/____/____
_____	_____	____/____/____
_____	_____	____/____/____
_____	_____	____/____/____
_____	_____	____/____/____

Do any of your relatives oppose your desire to live for God? _____ If yes, explain. _____

_____

Are you facing any current family crisis (separation, divorce, terminal illness, etc.)? _____ If yes, explain. _____

_____

_____

GENERAL INFORMATION

Occupation _____ Business phone _____

Spouse's Occupation _____ Business phone _____

Record other information about yourself that would help your discipler understand you better and pray for you more specifically. _____

_____

Your Bible study leader _____ Date _____

(Please photocopy and give to your Bible study leader when completed.)

LIVING THE EXCHANGE COMMITMENT

I am committing myself to faithfully attend each Bible study and also to pray for my fellow classmates for the following twelve weeks.

Signature _____

CLASS PRAYER LIST

_____

_____

_____

_____

_____

_____

_____

_____

_____

_____

_____

LESSON 1

MY NEW INHERITANCE

UNDERSTANDING WHAT I INHERITED
WHEN I RECEIVED CHRIST

When you received Jesus Christ as your own personal Savior, you inherited a lot more than you probably realized at the time. The Bible teaches

1. He **has** saved you from the **penalty** of sin, which is eternity in the lake of fire.

2. He currently **is** saving you from the **power** of sin, which until now has kept you from being able to break away from sinful living or even wanting to.

3. He **will** save you from the very **presence** of sin by giving you an eternal home in heaven.

The first and the last of these gifts are automatic and were completely settled the moment you made your great transaction with God by trusting Jesus to save you. The gift of victory over the **power** of sin was also "bequeathed" ("to leave to another by will") to you at that same moment, but you access it now by taking steps of faith. You might say that it is in your spiritual "bank account," but you must continually decide to "write the checks" against your account in order to have its full benefit.

The story is told of a wounded Civil War veteran who was known for talking about his friend "Mr. Lincoln" as he wandered from place to place begging because he could no longer work. When challenged by a stranger to prove that he really knew the beloved president, he reached into his wallet and pulled out a tattered piece of paper. He was embarrassed to admit, "I'm not much for reading, but I know that is Mr. Lincoln's signature." When the stranger read the tattered paper, he discovered that it was a generous federal pension, personally signed by Mr. Lincoln. He was walking around as a beggar though President Lincoln had met his every need. As a Christian there is no need for you to live spiritually bankrupt. Jesus has made the perfect provision for your spiritual inheritance.

This inheritance was given to you through the great exchange Jesus made for you on the cross. He took your death penalty upon Himself and gave you His eternal life. He took your sins and gave you His righteousness.

These gifts are actually byproducts of the very life of Jesus. You now have "Christ in you, the hope of glory" (Colossians 1:27). You have a new life and that new life is His life. The apostle Paul said his old life was crucified with Jesus; nevertheless, he was still alive, but it wasn't him that continued to live "but Christ [lives] in me"

(Galatians 2:20). *Living the Exchange* is about living out of the resources of His life and learning how to invest your inherited resources in God's invisible, eternal kingdom.

1. What did Jesus become in your place and what did you receive as a result?

    *2 Corinthians 8:9—For [you] know the grace of our Lord Jesus Christ, that, though he was rich, yet for your sakes **he became poor, that [you]** through his poverty **might be rich.***

    _____

    _____

2. When Paul prayed for the Christians in Ephesus, what three invisible realities were the people of Ephesus missing?

    *Ephesians 1:18–19—The eyes of your understanding being enlightened; that [you] may know what is **the hope of his calling,** and what **the riches** of the glory **of his inheritance** in the saints, And what is **the exceeding greatness of his power to us-ward** who believe, according to the working of his mighty power.*

    _____

    _____

The vastness of your inheritance is overwhelming. Drawing upon the inherited riches of Christ is not just your responsibility, but it is your privilege. Notice these pictures of living out of the resources of the exchange we have made with Jesus.

    Isaiah 12:3—Therefore with joy shall [you] draw water out of the wells of salvation.

    John 7:38–39a—He that [believes] on me [Jesus], as the scripture [has] said, out of his belly shall flow rivers of living water. (But this [spoke] he of the Spirit, which they that believe on him should receive.)

In this lesson we will look at three aspects of your inheritance in Christ and how you can come into full possession of all that is rightfully yours in Christ Jesus.

YOUR POSITIONAL STANDING

The word *positional* implies that our standing was given to us rather than personally earned. The word *standing* indicates that this is where we stand in our relationship with God. The blood of Jesus **has saved** you from the **penalty of sin** (eternity apart from Him in hell) and **has given** you a perfect standing with God through Christ's credited righteousness.

3. Will those who have chosen to depend on God for eternal life ever face condemnation?

    *John 5:24—Verily, Verily [Truly, truly], I [Jesus] say unto you, He that [hears] my word, and [believes] on him that sent me, [has] everlasting life, **and shall not come into condemnation; but is passed from death unto life.***

    _____

Why?

_____

4. Write the promise of God found in the following verses:

*Romans 4:5—But to him that [works] not, but [believes] on him that [justifies] the ungodly, **his faith is counted for righteousness**.*

_____

*2 Corinthians 5:21—For he [God has] made him [Jesus] to be sin for us, who knew no sin; that we might **be made the righteousness of God in him**.*

_____

Based on this promise, when we take His offer, we receive His righteous account and meet His holy standard.

This chart from *The Exchange* Bible study shows this exchange:

_____'s Record	Jesus' Record
Lying	Holy
Stealing	Just
Coveting	Accepted by God
Other sins	Free to live with God

Write your name in the blank above. Now cross out your name and write "Jesus." Cross out Jesus' name and write your own.

That is the reality of the exchange He gave you! He suffered as a lying, coveting thief in your place and offers you the ability to have a full relationship with God as your Father, accepted by Him because of Jesus' holy, just nature.

5. Read the following passage about Abraham, an Old Testament saint.

*Romans 4:21–25—**Being fully persuaded** that, what he had promised, he was able also to perform. And therefore it was imputed to him [credited to his account] for righteousness. Now it was not written for his sake alone, that it was imputed to him; but for us also, to whom it shall be imputed, if we believe on him that raised up Jesus our Lord from the dead; who was delivered for our offenses, and was raised again for our justification.*

How secure is your standing with God?

_____

What is required to have God's righteousness credited to your account?

Now it was not written for his sake alone, that it was imputed to him; but for us also, to whom it shall be imputed, **if we believe on him** *that raised up Jesus our Lord from the dead*

_____

What did Jesus do to give you this standing with God?

who was delivered for our offenses, and was raised again for our justification.

_____

This perfect standing with God is real and very valuable to you. Having "imputed" righteousness means that when God looks at you, He sees the perfect righteousness of Jesus instead of the sinful record you have earned through your actions. Your positional standing is the foundation for the practical success God provides to give you victory over sin as you obey Him.

YOUR PRACTICAL SUCCESS

The blood of Jesus **is saving** you from the power of sin and **is giving** you His grace to obey God's Word and thus live apart from sinning. The power of sin is the domination of sin over your life. Grace is God's supernatural enabling through His indwelling Spirit.

THE FUTILITY OF MY SELF—UNDERSTANDING THE INABILITY OF MY FLESH TO PLEASE GOD

6. Note the true state of man's nature without Christ.

    Romans 3:10–12—As it is written, There is **none righteous,** *no, not one: there is none that [understands], there is none that [seeks] after God. They are all gone out of the way, they are together become unprofitable; there is none that [does] good, no, not one.*

    How much righteousness is in man's nature?

    _____

    Does anyone have the ability to understand what God expects of him?

    there is **none that [understands]**

    _____

    Who seeks after God on his own?

    there is **none that [seeks] after God.**

    _____

Is there anyone who has the innate ability to look good in God's eyes?

They are all gone out of the way, **they are together become unprofitable;** *there is none that [does] good, no, not one.*

_____

7. Can we please God through our own abilities?

   Romans 8:8—So then **they that are in the flesh cannot please God.**

_____

In the New Testament the word *flesh* usually refers to the abilities of our human nature, not just the body in which we live. These "fleshly" abilities are often contrasted with the abilities we have when we are supernaturally enabled by God's Holy Spirit. "It is the Spirit that [quickens (gives life)]; the flesh [profits] nothing" (John 6:63*a*). **This supernatural enabling is called "grace."** Just as God gave us the ability to go to heaven simply by choosing to depend on Him, He is also willing to give us the ability to overcome the futility of our flesh.

THE FULLNESS OF MY SAVIOR—UNDERSTANDING THE PROMISE OF CHRIST'S LIFE IN YOU

8. Can we have victory over sin?

   Romans 6:14—For **sin shall not have dominion over [you]:** *for [you] are not under the law, but* **under grace.**

   Why or why not?

_____

9. What does God always promise to provide?

   2 Corinthians 2:14—Now thanks be unto God, which **always [causes] us to triumph in Christ,** *and [makes] manifest [clearly sensed] the savour [fragrance] of his knowledge by us in every place.*

_____

   In Whom?

_____

The first picture in this verse is of a Roman triumphal parade after a victory. When the Roman army won a battle in a distant land, they marched the spoils and sometimes even the captives of war down the streets of Rome to demonstrate their victory to the folk at home. Jesus has already won the victory for us through His death and resurrection. He now promises to put that victory on parade in our lives.

The second is the diffusing of the beautiful fragrance of Christ through our life. Though invisible, this powerful, invasive aura of God is His plan to show the world Who He is through our lives. Neither the victory, nor the beautiful fragrance is possible without Christ.

THE FOUNTAIN OF MY SURRENDER—APPROPRIATING THE POWER OF GOD FOR MY LIFE

10.   What two gifts are promised in this verse?

*Romans 5:1–2—Therefore being **justified by faith**, we have peace with God through our Lord Jesus Christ: by whom also we have **access by faith into this grace wherein we stand**, and rejoice in hope of the glory of God.*

_____

How do we access these?

_____

The word *hope* means eager expectation. Romans 3:23 teaches that sin causes all of us to "come short of the glory of God," but Romans 5:2 tells us that by continuing to exercise faith we can expect to see the glory of God demonstrated through our lives.

Verse 6 of the same chapter reminds us that we were "without strength" when Jesus found us. The phrase *much more* is used five times in Romans 5 referring to the abundant, abounding grace God has given us in His ongoing work of salvation. The gift of His own life in exchange for ours is the source of the abounding grace displayed in this wonderful chapter.

11.   Remember the picture of drawing from the wells of salvation. What had the people of Jeremiah's day done?

*Jeremiah 2:13—For my people have committed two evils; **they have forsaken me** the fountain of living waters, and hewed them out cisterns, broken cisterns, that can hold no water.*

_____

God wanted to supply them with His abounding grace. Not only had they stopped depending on Him as their source of life but they had begun to look to their own resources, which were not capable of genuine supply. We will see that our surrendering and depending through steps of faith are the means by which we draw from the fountain of God's enabling grace.

- **The Surrender of Faith**—Trusting God enough to surrender your life to Him

12.   An Old Testament sacrifice meant the death of an animal. What kind of sacrifice is God asking from you today?

*Romans 12:1—I beseech you therefore, [brothers], by the mercies of God, that [you] present your bodies a **living sacrifice, holy, acceptable unto God**, which is your reasonable service.*

_____

Note the words *holy* and *acceptable unto God*. Only God is holy. We are responsible to take steps of faith toward holy living, but we can live holy lives in this lifetime only by **surrendering** to Him and **depending** on Him to live His holiness in us. Just as He gave us grace for eternal life at salvation, He now gives us grace for holy living. The word *acceptable* means well-pleasing. Hebrews 11:6 teaches us that "without faith it is impossible to please him." God has given *"the exceeding greatness of his power to us-ward"* who believe (Ephesians 1:19), but we experience His power in our lives only as we give Him the right to rule as Lord over our lives.

Many people want to use God as a servant or a genie to manipulate and use for their own desires. That's not the way it works. When we yield ourselves to **Him** to be used as **His** servant, **then** He is ready to enable us do what **He** desires. Are you willing to surrender your life to Him and live as His servant? This is crucial if you are to see His strength living in you.

- **The Continuation of Faith**—Choosing to surrender and depend on a moment-by-moment basis

13. How does He expect us to live once we have surrendered to Him?

    *Hebrews 10:38—Now the just shall **live by faith**: but if any man draw back, my soul shall have no pleasure in him.*

    _____

THE FILLING OF MY SPIRIT—EXPERIENCING THE REALITIES OF GOD'S GRACE IN MY LIFE

14. Who lives in us now that we are saved?

    *1 Corinthians 6:19—What? [Don't you know] that your body is the temple of the **Holy Spirit** which is in you, which [you] have of God, and [you] are not your own?*

    _____

Ephesians 5:18 teaches that just as alcohol controls the person who is drunk, the Holy Spirit will control the person who is "filled" with Him. "And be not drunk with wine, wherein is excess; but be filled with the Spirit."

THE FRUITFULNESS OF MY SERVICE—FULFILLING THE PURPOSE OF THE SPIRIT-FILLED LIFE—SERVICE FOR THE KING

15. What is the purpose for God's grace?

    *2 Corinthians 9:8—And God is able to make all grace abound toward you; that [you], always having all sufficiency in all things, **may abound to every good work**.*

    _____

Sanctification is the process of God making you more and more holy like Himself. This process began the day you received Christ as your personal Savior and will continue for the rest of your lifetime. God is committed to your sanctification because you belong to Him. In fact Romans 8 teaches that your sanctification is the focus of His current work in your life. He will never stop this work until you have been perfectly remade and receive your "glorified" body in heaven.

YOUR PERMANENT SANCTUARY

In a wildlife sanctuary the animals are not exposed to the dangers to which the animals outside the sanctuary are exposed. When we get to heaven, we will permanently be protected from the dangers of sin and its effects. The blood of Jesus **will save** you from the very presence of sin and **will give** you an eternal home with Him in glory!

16. Where did Jesus say He was going?

    *John 14:1–3—Let not your heart be troubled: [you] believe in God, believe also in me. **In my Father's house** are many mansions: if it were not so, I would have told you. **I go to prepare a place for you**. And if **I go and prepare a place for you**, I will come again, and receive you unto myself; that where I am, there [you] may be also.*

What did He say He was preparing for those who believe in Him?

_____

17. Where does the believer go as soon as his body dies?

   *2 Corinthians 5:8—We are confident, I say, and willing rather to be absent from the body, and to be **present with the Lord**.*

_____

The Bible teaches us in 1 Corinthians 15:53–55 that God is going to give us new incorruptible bodies in heaven. Revelation 21:3–4 teaches us that God Himself will wipe away all tears. He plans to do away with death, pain, and sorrow, all of which have their origin in sin. Praise the Lord, friend, if you have placed your trust in Christ, someday God will give you a new sinless body and put you in a place without sin with Him forever.

18. Are you 100 percent sure that all your sins are forgiven and that you're going to heaven?

   _____ Yes _____ No   If you answered yes, in the space provided on page 9 of this lesson, please explain how you came to this knowledge. This story is called your testimony.

APPLICATION

God promises His special blessings to those who will act on what He teaches in His Word.

   *James 1:22–25—But **be . . . doers of the word**, and not hearers only, deceiving your own selves. For if any be a hearer of the word, and not a doer, he is like unto a man beholding his natural face in a glass [mirror]: for he [beholds] himself, and [goes] his way, and straightway [forgets] what manner of man he was. But [whosoever looks] into the perfect law of liberty [the Bible], and [continues] therein, he being not a forgetful hearer, but a **doer of the work**, this man shall be blessed in his deed.*

In this lesson you have seen that God promises you His victory as you surrender your life to Him and begin taking steps of obedience in dependence on His promised strength to do His work. We will look more in depth at these issues in the lessons to come, but will you ask God to continue to make you willing to have Him work in your life to this end?

In the space below write your request in the form of a prayer.

_____

_____

_____

_____

ASSIGNMENTS

Bible Reading: John 1–7

Scripture Memory:

> *2 Corinthians 5:17—Therefore if any man be in Christ, he is a new creature: old things are passed away; behold, all things are become new.*

(This verse is part of *The Exchange* Scripture Memory System.)

Practical Assignment: Write your personal testimony.

_____

_____

_____

_____

_____

_____

_____

_____

_____

This week record one thing from each day's Bible reading God used to speak to your heart.

Day 1

_____

_____

Day 2

_____

_____

Day 3

_____

_____

_____

Day 4

_____

_____

_____

Day 5

_____

_____

_____

Day 6

_____

_____

_____

Day 7

_____

_____

_____

LESSON 2

MY BIBLE

UNDERSTANDING THE FOUNDATIONAL NATURE OF THE WORD OF GOD

Before we continue our study about living out of the inherited resources of our regenerated spirit, let's look at the role the Bible plays in the victory God's promises. The dominating desire of a newborn is for his mother's milk, which contains all the nourishment a baby needs for strength and growth. This is a great picture of what the Word of God is to a growing Christian. All that is needed for spiritual strength and growth in every area of life is found in the Bible. A healthy Christian hungers after and feeds regularly on the Word of God. A working knowledge of the Bible and a submissive dependence on the Bible are absolutely necessary for spiritual life and growth. Study this lesson carefully. It will lead you to a healthy appreciation of the Bible and a vibrant approach to gaining its spiritual nourishment.

WHAT IS THE BIBLE?

The Bible is the complete, authoritative revelation of God's person and truth to mankind. It is all we need to know about Who God is, who we are, and how we can have a right relationship with God.

1. What is God's Word?

    *John 17:17—**Sanctify them** through [Your] truth: [**Your] word is truth.***

    _____

    What does it do?

    _____

This verse is from the last recorded prayer of Jesus before His crucifixion. The word *sanctify* means to set apart for a special use. Jesus asked God to use the Bible as the means by which His followers might be made holy for His service. When He declares the Bible to be truth, He declares it as the absolute last word in any matter. The Bible is so complete that God promises great judgment upon the person who attacks it.

2. What are the two things God warns all men not to do to His Word?

*Revelation 22:18–19—For I testify unto every man that [hears] the words of the prophecy of this book, If any man shall **add unto these things**, God shall add unto him the plagues that are written in this book: and if any man shall **take away from the words of the book of this prophecy**, God shall take away his part out of the book of life, and out of the holy city, and from the things which are written in this book.*

_____

It is important to remember that when a person receives God's gift of eternal life, he has "passed from death unto life" and will "not come into condemnation" (John 5:24). This passage in Revelation does not teach that one can lose his eternal salvation, but it clearly shows God's attitude toward tampering with His Word. If a man purposely chooses to disregard a particular truth from the Bible, he is guilty before God. It is imperative to have a healthy respect for the absolute authority of God's Word.

3. What does the Bible say about God's credibility?

*Titus 1:2—In hope of eternal life, which **God**, that **cannot lie**, promised before the world began.*

_____

There are going to be times when what you read in the Bible doesn't seem to be true based on what you are experiencing. Our limited view is not be the final judge of truth. It is important at such times to remember that the Bible is the definer of truth. Learn to judge your circumstances in the light of the Bible and not judge the Bible in the light of your circumstances. Our emotions also deceive us at times and make us **feel** that the Word of God is not true. The great reformer Martin Luther wrote this poem to remind himself of the reliability of the Bible versus his own emotions.

> *Feelings come and feelings go,*
> *And feelings are deceiving;*
> *My warrant is the Word of God*
> *Naught else is worth believing.*

Setting up your experiences as your guide leads to living like a butterfly, flitting from experience to experience, never knowing where they will take you. It is better to use the Bible as your roadmap and follow its leadership. You will still have a lifetime of great experiences, but all the while you will be growing deeper and deeper in your relationship with God.

4. The Bible is described in many terms. Find the following word comparisons in the verses below and circle each one. Take a moment with each verse to consider how the Bible and the object compare to each other.

Fire/Sword/Mirror/Lamp/Milk

Meat/Seed/Hammer/Water/Light

Circle the answers (what should be in bold) if you can.

*Psalm 119:105—Thy **word** is a **lamp** unto my feet, and a **light** unto my path.*

*Ephesians 5:26—That he might sanctify and cleanse it with the washing of **water** by the **word**.*

*Jeremiah 23:29—Is not my **word** like as a **fire**? says the Lord; and like a **hammer** that breaks the rock in pieces?*

*1 Peter 2:2—As newborn babes, desire the sincere **milk** of the **Word**, that [you] may grow thereby.*

*Hebrews 4:12—For the **word of God** is quick [alive], and powerful [effective], and sharper than any twoedged **sword**, piercing even to the dividing asunder of soul and spirit, and of the joints and marrow, and is a discerner of the thoughts and intents of the heart.*

*James 1:23–24—For if any be a hearer of the **word**, and not a doer, he is like unto a man beholding his natural face in a **glass** [mirror]: for he [beholds] himself, and [goes] his way, and straightway [forgets] what manner of man he was.*

*1 Peter 1:23—Being born again, not of corruptible **seed**, but of incorruptible, by the **word of God**, which [lives] and [abides] for ever.*

*Ephesians 6:17—And take the helmet of salvation, and the **sword** of the Spirit, which is the **word of God**.*

*1 Corinthians 3:2—I have fed you with **milk**, and not with **meat**.*

5. What purpose for the Bible is revealed in each of the following passages?

*2 Timothy 3:15—From a child [you have] known the holy scriptures, which are **able to make [you] wise unto salvation** through faith which is in Christ Jesus.*

_____

*2 Timothy 3:17—That the man of God may **be perfect, thoroughly furnished unto all good works**.*

_____

*2 Corinthians 3:18—But we all, with open face **beholding** as in a glass **the glory of the Lord, are changed into the same image** from glory to glory, even as by the Spirit of the Lord.*

_____

6. How long will the Word of God last?

*1 Peter 1:23—Being born again, not of corruptible seed, but of incorruptible, by **the word of God**, which [lives] and **[abides] for ever**.*

_____

HOW DID WE GET OUR BIBLE?

7. Who controlled the men who spoke and wrote the Scriptures?

*2 Peter 1:21—For the prophecy came not in old time by the will of man: but holy men of God [spoke] as they were **moved by the Holy Ghost**.*

_____

8. How much of the Bible is inspired?

*2 Timothy 3:16—**All Scripture is given by inspiration of God**, and is profitable for doctrine, for reproof, for correction, for instruction in righteousness.*

_____

The Bible uses the word *inspiration* to describe how we got our Bible. *Inspiration* means "God-breathed." Just as air is breathed out of living creatures, so the words of Scripture flowed directly out of the living God. Inspiration is the supernatural process by which God used men to write down without error the exact words God chose to communicate His truth to mankind.

KNOWING AND DEPENDING ON THE BIBLE

9. Circle the four ways in which the Bible is profitable.

    2 Timothy 3:16—All Scripture is given by inspiration of God, and is profitable for doctrine, for reproof, for correction, for instruction in righteousness.

The word *doctrine* means teachings. The Bible teaches us what is true, points out our disobedience to the truth, helps us make necessary corrections, and then shows us how to stay right.

10. Record the words that describe the life of a person who knows and gives himself to the truth of the Bible.

    *Joshua 1:8—This book of the law shall not depart out of [your] mouth; but [you shall] meditate therein day and night, that [you may] observe to do according to all that is written therein: for then [you shall] make [your] way **prosperous**, and then [you shall] have **good success**.*

    _____

    *Psalm 1:2–3—But his delight is in the law of the Lord; and in his law [does] he meditate day and night. And he shall be like **a tree planted by the rivers** of water, that [**brings**] **forth his fruit** in his season; **his leaf also shall not wither**; and [**whatever he does**] **shall prosper**.*

    _____

11. How valuable is the Word of God?

    *Psalm 19:10—**More to be desired** are they **than gold**, yea, than much fine gold: **sweeter** also **than honey** and the honeycomb.*

    _____

12. How did the earth and the heavens get here?

    *2 Peter 3:5—**By the word of God** the heavens were of old, and the earth.*

    _____

Though the Word of God referred to in this verse is God's spoken voice, the words of God recorded in the Bible are from the same source and have the same creative life-giving effect on our lives.

13. What is the most important reason God wrote the Bible?

    *John 20:31—But **these are written, that [you] might believe** that Jesus is the Christ, the Son of God; and that believing [you] might have life through his name.*

    _____

    *Romans 10:17—So then **faith [comes] by hearing, and hearing by the word of God**.*

    _____

14. What is necessary to please God?

    *Hebrews 11:6—But without **faith** it is impossible to please him.*

    _____

Faith is not simply understanding something and agreeing that it is true. It is choosing to personally depend on that truth. We can please the Lord only by genuinely believing the Bible. Obedience is simply the necessary result of depending on its truth.

Jesus is clearly called "the Word" in two different places and is equated with "the Word" in many others.

15. What did Jesus call Himself, and what did He say men must do to experience His life in them?

    *John 6:51—I am **the living bread** which came down from heaven: if any man **eat of this bread**, he shall live for ever: and the bread that I will give is my flesh, which I will give for the life of the world.*

    _____

Jesus is the living Word and the Bible is the written Word; in a sense you are partaking of Jesus when you choose to read and believe the Bible.

It is not enough to look at bread. You must eat it before it is beneficial. It is not enough for you to simply read the Bible or listen to others talk about it. You must choose to rely on it for yourself before you can experience its benefits.

HOW TO STUDY THE BIBLE

16. How often should you study the Bible?

    *Joshua 1:8—This book of the law shall not depart out of [your] mouth; but **[you shall] meditate therein day and night**, that [you may] observe to do according to all that is written therein: for then [you shall] make [your] way prosperous, and then [you shall] have good success.*

    _____

    In your own words write what it means to meditate.

    _____

    _____

    _____

Some might say that meditation is emptying your mind of everything and letting an inner voice speak to you. In this verse the thought is to purposely think about or contemplate the truth from God's Word. While it is true that God's Spirit leads us in this activity, it is necessary to realize that He does so using the words of Scripture. He expects our mind to actively, not passively, pursue His truth.

17. Why should you memorize God's Word?

*Psalm 119:9–11—Wherewithal shall a young **man cleanse his way**? By taking heed thereto according to [your] word. With my whole heart have I sought thee: O let me not wander from [your] commandments. [Your] word have I hid in mine heart, **that I might not sin against thee**.*

_____

18. What word picture is used to describe memorizing the Bible?

*James 1:21—Wherefore lay apart all filthiness and superfluity [abundance] of naughtiness, and receive with meekness the **engrafted word**, which is able to save your souls.*

_____

The picture of the engrafted Word is that of a grapevine or a fruit tree with a new branch grafted in. The new branch becomes an actual part of the living plant and allows the old plant to bear the good fruit of the engrafted branch. God wants us to literally graft His Word right into the very fabric of the way we think and, thus, begin to change the fruit we bear.

19. How does God want us to approach the Word of God?

*1 Peter 2:2–3—As newborn babes, **desire the sincere milk of the word**, that you may grow thereby: if so be you have tasted that the Lord is gracious.*

_____

20. Can the Bible mean one thing to one person and something totally different to another?

*2 Peter 1:20–21—Knowing this first, that **no prophecy of the scripture is of any private interpretation. For the prophecy came not in old time by the will of man**: but holy men of God [spoke] as they were moved by the Holy [Spirit].*

_____

Why?

_____

The phrase "private interpretation" mentioned in this verse is not aimed at the reader so much as it is a record of how the Bible got to us. The Bible is not the private opinions of human writers but the revelation of God. As such, there is a message from God that must be discovered without putting our own ideas or thoughts into it. Because it is not a human book, we can't take what we want and discard the rest. It is a divine book, and God promises divine (supernatural) abilities through the faith it produces in its followers.

21. What does God promise to those who step out on His promises?

*2 Peter 1:4—Whereby are given unto us exceeding great and precious promises: that by these **[you] might be partakers of the divine nature**, having escaped the corruption that is in the world through lust.*

_____

22. Who must we depend upon to help us understand the meaning of the Scripture?

*1 Corinthians 2:12–13—Now we have received, not the spirit of the world, but **the spirit** which is of God; that we might know the things that are freely given to us of God. Which things also we speak, not in the words which man's wisdom [teaches], but which the **Holy [Spirit** teaches]; comparing spiritual things with spiritual.*

_____

Some have called this illumination. It is as if the words He wants us to understand and apply to our lives are illumined and sometimes seem to jump off the page at us. Each time you get alone with your Bible allows you an intimate moment alone with God. As you spend time with God in your Bible, you will be growing in your relationship with Him. Don't forget! God is not a concept to learn about. He is a person to get to know intimately!

APPLICATION

23. James 1:22–25 teaches that we must not just be a hearer of the Word but also a doer of the Word. Note the picture here. What does God teach that you must do before you receive the blessing of the Word of God?

*James 1:22–25—But be . . . doers of the word, and not hearers only, deceiving your own selves. For if any be a hearer of the word, and not a doer, he is like unto a man beholding his natural face in a glass [mirror]: for he [beholds] himself, and [goes] his way, and straightway [forgets] what manner of man he was. But whoso ª[**looks] into the perfect law of liberty**, and ᵇ[**continues] therein**, he ᶜ**being not a forgetful hearer**, ᵈ**but a doer of the work**, this man shall be blessed in his deed.*

You have learned that the Bible is the foundation of your Christian life. It is through the Bible that God will speak to you the rest of your life. No doubt God wants you to make some decisions about your attitudes and actions toward His Word. Would you bow your head and ask Him to lead your heart to those changes? Maybe He desires for you to carve out a time daily to read the Bible, or maybe He wants you to commit to memorize your Bible verses. It may be that He wants you to be hungrier for His Word or to see it as absolute, not relative truth. Perhaps He is burdening you to be in church regularly to hear His Word taught and applied to your daily living. Has God tugged at your heart concerning any of these issues? Perhaps you should look back over the lesson and allow Him to remind you of anything else.

Write a prayer to God expressing your resolve concerning the areas He has revealed to you.

_____

_____

_____

ASSIGNMENTS

Bible Reading: John 8–14

Scripture Memory:

Psalm 119:9–11—Wherewithal shall a young man cleanse his way? By taking heed thereto according to [Your] word. With my whole heart have I sought [You]: O let me not wander from [your] commandments. [Your] word have I hid in mine heart, that I might not sin against [You].

(This verse is part of *The Exchange* Scripture Memory System.)

Practical Assignment: Read Matthew 4:1–11.

With what three words did Jesus begin each of His answers to Satan's temptation?

_____

As you grow to know God's Word and draw nourishment from it, you are growing to know and draw nourishment from God Himself.

In the appendix at the end of the book you will find a reading schedule in which you can mark the passages you have read in the Bible. If you read last week's Bible reading (John 1–7), mark it on the schedule.

As you read John 8–14, the following questions will assist you in personally applying the truth of God to your own life:

- What part of God's glory is revealed in this passage?

- Are there any promises I can claim?

- Are there any commands I should obey?

- Are there any principles I should apply?

- Is there any sin I should forsake?

- Are there any examples I should follow?

- Are there any warnings I should heed?

This week record one thing from each day's Bible reading God used to speak to your heart.

Day 1

_____

_____

Day 2

_____

_____

Day 3

_____

_____

Day 4

_____

_____

Day 5

_____

_____

Day 6

_____

_____

Day 7

_____

_____

Start recording any questions you may encounter from your Bible reading. Feel free to discuss them with your Bible study leader. Look over the chart in the appendix of all the books of the Bible and ask your Bible study leader any questions you may have concerning it.

See pages 129–130 for additional information

LESSON 3

MY BAPTISM AND CHURCH MEMBERSHIP

UNDERSTANDING PUBLIC IDENTIFICATION WITH CHRIST AND JOINING A BIBLE-BELIEVING CHURCH

Congratulations on your decision to receive Christ's exchange! The decision itself was completely voluntary and private, but it is impossible to keep such a decision hidden. In fact, God has designed a public identification with Jesus that not only allows you to show others what He has done in your life but also aligns you with others who have made the same decision. This public identification is baptism, and the ongoing alignment is church membership. The Bible teaches that when you became a Christian, you immediately became a child of God. You are now part of a family of believers. God is your Father, and all other Christians are your brothers and sisters in Christ. God's plan for each of His children is to have a home where he or she receives and gives encouragement to live for Him. This lesson is about that public identification and how to choose, join, and function within a church home for you and your family.

THE MEANING AND IMPORTANCE OF BAPTISM

The New Testament was originally written in Greek and was later translated into English. The word *baptize* is a transliteration of the Greek word *bap-tid-zo*. The translators created an English word from the Greek word rather than give its meaning, which is "to dip, to immerse, to place under, or to overwhelm." Baptism is a picture of being placed into the death, burial and resurrection of Christ. It is a testimony to others that you have been saved. Both baptism and faithful church attendance are imperative steps of obedience for the Christian.

1. What do the following verses say is necessary in order to be saved? Do the verses include baptism?

    *Romans 10:13—For whosoever shall **call upon the name of the Lord** shall be saved.*

    _____

    *Ephesians 2:8–9—For **by grace** are [you] saved **through faith**; and that not of yourselves: it is the gift of God: **not of works**, lest any man should boast.*

    _____

It is extremely important for believers to be baptized, but understand that it is a part of your walk with the Lord **after** you are saved.

2. Through what do we obtain forgiveness of sins?

   *Ephesians 1:7—In whom we have redemption **through his blood**, the forgiveness of sins, **according** to the riches of **his grace**.*

When Jesus was on earth, He left His disciples with instructions about what to do once He returned to heaven. These instructions are recorded in each of the first five books of the New Testament. His instructions have long been called the Great Commission because He commissioned every believer to these tasks. It is the purpose for the church, God's chosen body of believers, to do His work in this age. Matthew 28:18–20 gives the most detailed record of these instructions.

*Matthew 28:18–20—And Jesus came and [spoke] unto them, saying, [1]All power is given unto me in heaven and in earth. [2]**Go** therefore, and **teach all nations**, [3]**baptizing them** in the name of the Father, and of the Son, and of the Holy Ghost: [4]**teaching them to observe [obey]** all things whatsoever I have commanded you: [5]and, lo, I am with you alway, even unto the end of the world. Amen.*

The Great Commission has five basic elements:

- 1. Everything that men do, including work in the church, must be for the glory of God.

- 2–4. The three basic purposes of the church.

- 5. God receives the glory when His children obey these instructions by depending on His power and presence.

3. List the three basic purposes of the church found in Matthew 28:18–20.

The words translated "Go therefore, and teach all nations" can be stated, "Go to every people group in the world and make disciples or followers of Me by teaching them the way of salvation." Lesson 12 deals fully with this concept. The next main purpose of the church is to gather these converts into a body of believers who have all been identified as His followers through public baptism. The third purpose for the church is to train the believers to obey Jesus' teaching.

As a new believer you have already participated in the first important step of God's plan for this age! You have become a disciple, or follower, of Jesus. Now His plan is for you to continue on in the next two steps.

4. According to Matthew 28:18–20, what is the next step you need to take?

If you answered, "To become a part of a church body by being baptized," you are right. If you have already been scripturally baptized after your salvation, then your next step is to join a Bible-preaching church. If you are currently a member of a Bible-preaching church, your next step is to become actively involved in helping fulfill the Great Commission in your church. The questions remain "What is baptism? What does it mean?"

Romans 6 deals with spiritual baptism and is a crucial passage when considering these questions. Spiritual baptism is the act of being placed into the spiritual body of Jesus. Through Him we have already experienced the benefits of His death and resurrection. Physical baptism is a picture of spiritual baptism.

5. How does this external picture show the internal event that has already taken place in your heart?

    Romans 6:3–5—Know [you] not, that so many of us as were **baptized** *[placed]* **into Jesus Christ** *were* **baptized** *[placed]* **into his death**? *Therefore we are* **buried with him by baptism** *[immersion]* **into death**: *that like as Christ was* **raised up from the dead** *by the glory of the Father, even so we also should walk in newness of life. For if we have been* **planted together in the likeness of his death**, *we shall be also* **in the likeness of his resurrection**.

    _____

Baptism is being placed into the body of Christ through the death, burial, and resurrection of Jesus. Which mode of baptism—sprinkling or immersion—would best show this picture? Obviously, the picture is immersion, in which a believer is placed under the water and then raised back out.

6. Why did John choose this particular place to baptize?

    John 3:23—And John also was baptizing in Aenon near to Salim, **because there was much water there**: *and they came, and were baptized.*

    _____

7. The book of Acts records the beginning of the church. In the following verses note who was baptized and what preceded their baptism.

    Acts 2:41—Then **they** *that* **gladly received his word** *were baptized: and the same day there were added unto them about three thousand souls.*

    _____

    Acts 8:12—But when **they believed Philip preaching** *the things concerning the kingdom of God, and the name of Jesus Christ, they were baptized, both men and women.*

    _____

    Acts 8:36–38—And as they went on their way, they came unto a certain water: and the eunuch said, See, here is water; what [does] hinder me to be baptized? And Philip said, **If [you believe] with all [your] heart**, *[you may]. And he answered and said, I believe that Jesus Christ is the Son of God. And he commanded the chariot to stand still: and they went down both into the water, both Philip and the eunuch; and he baptized him.*

    _____

    Acts 10:46–48—Then answered Peter, Can any man forbid water, that these should not be baptized, **which have received the Holy [Spirit]** *as well as we? And he commanded them to be baptized in the name of the Lord.*

    [Remember, the Holy Spirit indwells only believers.]

    _____

*Acts 16:30–33—And [he] brought them out, and said, Sirs, what must I do to be saved? And they said, **Believe on the Lord Jesus Christ, and [you shall] be saved**, and [your] house. And they [spoke] unto him the word of the Lord, and to all that were in his house. And he took them the same hour of the night, and washed their stripes [wounds from being whipped]; and was baptized.*

_____

What pattern do you notice?

_____

8. According to these Scriptures, how soon after salvation were people baptized?

_____

Many were baptized the same day they were saved. The longest time between salvation and baptism recorded in the Bible is three days (the apostle Paul—Acts 9:1–18). If you have been saved, nothing should keep you from being baptized.

9. Have you been scripturally baptized according to these Scriptures since you were saved?

_____

10. If baptism is a command from the Lord, what would you call refusal to be baptized?

*James 4:17—Therefore to him that [knows] to do good, and [does] it not, to him **it is sin**.*

_____

Baptism is gladly identifying with Jesus. One might liken it to wearing a wedding ring. When I got married, my wife gave me a simple gold wedding band. I wear it to identify myself as belonging to her. The vows we made before God and men joined us. The ring is simply a symbol that the marriage took place. I don't wear the ring to get married. I wear it to show that I am married. What if I put the ring on my teenage son? What would it mean on his finger? Nothing! He's not married yet. In a similar way, baptism is a picture of our union with Christ at salvation. If a person were baptized before salvation, it is as meaningless as my son's wearing my wedding ring. **Salvation must precede baptism for baptism to mean anything.** What if I took my ring off? Would I be unmarried? No! The ring doesn't make me married. It shows others that I am married. In a similar way, if a person doesn't get baptized, it doesn't make him unsaved. It makes him disobedient. What if I were to take my ring off and lay it on the table in front of my wife and curtly inform her that I wasn't going to wear it anymore? Do you think it would hurt my relationship with her? Yes! In a similar way, while not being baptized doesn't change your standing with God, it does damage your relationship with Him. God's perfect will for your life is that you show the world that you belong to Him by being baptized and becoming an active participant in a Bible-believing church family.

THE IMPORTANCE OF CHURCH MEMBERSHIP

Picture a log fire burning brightly in a cozy fireplace. Now imagine taking one of the logs out and setting it on the hearth. What do you think will happen? The log that was taken out will probably stop burning, start smoking, and make a mess. If you take the same log and put it back into the fireplace where it belongs, it will once again burn brightly and warm the room. In a similar way, God has built the local church to help you stay on fire and be of use to the Lord. Christians who get out of church lose their zeal and make a mess of God's plan for their lives. Christians who stay in church as God intended are more likely to grow in their spiritual walk and usefulness to God.

Hebrews 10:21 teaches that Jesus is the ever-living leader of the church and His church family is called the house of God. The following passage lists some of the benefits and responsibilities of being a part of this family.

> *Hebrews 10:22–25—*^a*Let us draw near with a true heart in full assurance of faith, having our hearts sprinkled from an evil conscience, and our bodies washed with pure water.* ^b*Let us hold fast the profession of our faith without wavering; (for he is faithful that promised;) and let us consider one another to provoke unto love and to good works: not forsaking the assembling of ourselves together, as the manner of some is; but exhorting [building up] one another: and so much the more, as [you] see the day approaching.*

11. In your own words describe the two benefits of a strong church family listed in the first two parts of this passage.

    a.

    _____

    b.

    _____

Actively participating in a local church promotes changing the way we view sin and promotes restoring a healthy conscience. It helps us clean up our lives to more accurately show Jesus to the world in which we live. It gives us the ability to become consistent in our Christian living by learning to obey God in dependence on His promises and on the Promise Giver.

12. In your own words, describe a church member's responsibilities in the second two parts of Hebrews 10:22–25.

    > *And* ^c*let us consider one another to provoke unto love and to good works:* ^d*not forsaking the assembling of ourselves together, as the manner of some is; but exhorting [building up] one another: and so much the more, as [you] see the day approaching.*

    c.

    _____

    d.

    _____

You know what it means to provoke someone to frustration. Consider a place where everyone provokes one another to love and good works. It is probable that not everyone in any church lives this way, but the emphasis is on our being that kind of person in our local church. The responsibility continues, teaching us that we need to faithfully attend church so that we can build up one another. The closer we get to the Lord's return, the more important our participation in our local church family becomes.

13. How often do you think the Lord would have you attend church?

    _____

Most Bible-preaching churches have three or more services a week. The more you attend, the more opportunities you give yourself for spiritual growth and maturity. Church not only helps us grow in the Lord but is God's plan for reaching the world with the gospel. Only through the local church can we be obedient to God's Great Commission, which is the purpose of the church. We must all join and participate in the programs of a Bible-preaching local church in order to fulfill this commission.

14. In the first church what immediately followed salvation and baptism?

*Acts 2:41—Then they that gladly received his word were baptized: and the same day there **were added unto them** about three thousand souls.*

_____

Church membership is available only to people who have been saved and baptized. In fact, the act of baptism placed these first believers into the church.

15. List the four activities of the early church.

*Acts 2:42—And they continued steadfastly in the apostles' **doctrine** and **fellowship**, and in **breaking of bread**, and in **prayers**.*

_____

_____

_____

- Steadfast—to adhere or be glued to, to be devoted to, regularly

- Doctrine—authoritative teaching

- Fellowship—intimate joint participation in a common community

- Breaking of bread—remembering the death and resurrection of the Lord

- Prayers—corporately approaching the throne of God

16. Of what dangers do you need to be careful when choosing a church?

*Galatians 1:6–9—I marvel that [you] are so soon removed from him that called you into the grace of Christ unto **another gospel**: which is not another; but there be some that trouble you, and **would pervert the gospel of Christ**. But though we, or an angel from heaven, **preach any other gospel** unto you than that which we have preached unto you, let him be accursed. As we said before, so say I now again, If any man **preach any other gospel** unto you than that you have received, let him be accursed.*

_____

*2 Timothy 4:3–4—For the time will come when **they will not endure sound doctrine**; but after their own lusts [desires] shall they heap to themselves **teachers, having itching ears**; and they shall **turn** away their ears **from the truth**, and shall **be turned unto fables**.*

_____

17. What two offices of leadership were given to the local church?

    *1 Timothy 3:1, 8—This is a true saying, If a man desire the office of a **bishop** [pastor], he desires a good work. . . . Likewise must the **deacons** . . The word bishop is one of three names given to the pastor in the Bible.*

18. For what purpose is the evangelist and pastor/teacher given to the church?

    *Ephesians 4:11–12—And he gave some, apostles; and some, prophets; and some, evangelists; and some, pastors and teachers; **for the perfecting [equipping] of the saints [believers]**, for [into] the work of the ministry, for the edifying [building up] of the body of Christ.*

    _____

19. What should be your attitude toward the leadership of the local church?

    *1 Thessalonians 5:12–13—And we beseech [plead with] you, brethren, to **know them** which labor among you, and are over you in the Lord, and admonish you; and to **esteem [value] them very highly in love** for their work's sake. And be at peace among yourselves.*

    _____

    *Hebrews 13:17—**Obey them** that have the rule over you, and **submit yourselves**: for they watch for your souls, as they that must give account, that they may do it with joy, and not with grief: for that is unprofitable for you.*

    _____

APPLICATION

James 1:22–25 promises God's special blessing on those who take action on what His Word teaches.

20. What is the main ministry of every Christian?

    *Acts 1:8—But [you] shall receive power, after that the Holy [Spirit] is come upon you: and **[you] shall be witnesses unto me** both in Jerusalem, and in all Judaea, and in Samaria, and unto the uttermost part of the earth.*

    _____

    *Mark 16:15—And he [Jesus] said unto them, **Go . . . into all the world, and preach the gospel** to every creature.*

    _____

21. Of what must you be a part before you are able to fulfill this Great Commission?

    _____

In this lesson you have seen that God's perfect plan for you is to join a local church by publicly identifying yourself with Him through baptism. If you have never been scripturally baptized, are you willing to do so now? If you have already been baptized, are you willing to join and actively participate in a Bible-preaching church?

Write your resolve to obey in a prayer.

_____

_____

_____

_____

_____

_____

_____

_____

If you are not willing to obey, write the reason you are procrastinating. Also write the consequences that will result from not obeying.

_____

_____

_____

_____

ASSIGNMENTS

Bible Reading: John 15–21

Scripture Memory:

> _Hebrews 10:24–25—And let us consider one another to provoke unto love and to good works: not forsaking the assembling of ourselves together, as the manner of some is; but exhorting one another: and so much the more, as [you] see the day approaching._

(This verse is part of _The Exchange_ Scripture Memory System.)

Practical Assignment: Ask your Bible study leader to help you talk to the pastor about your decision to be baptized and join the church.

In the space below write in your own words why you are glad you became a Christian and want to show the world you belong to Jesus.

_____

_____

_____

_____

What ministries in the church do you believe God may be stirring your heart to investigate?

_____

_____

_____

_____

Ask your Bible study leader to introduce you to the leaders of these ministries.

_____

_____

_____

LESSON 4

THE FUTILITY OF MY SELF

UNDERSTANDING THE INABILITY OF THE FLESH TO PLEASE GOD

We have seen an overview of our inheritance, including the gift of God's infallible Word, which is sufficient to meet our every need. Lessons 4–7 will add some details concerning our need and appropriation of our inheritance. Lessons 8–11 will deal with a few critical areas of life in which we can count on this inheritance to enable us. This lesson is the bad news, but it is necessary to see the futility of our flesh before we will be serious about looking to God's promised presence in our lives. As you complete this lesson, please remember what Christ promises us in 2 Corinthians 12:9: "My grace is sufficient for [you] for my strength is made perfect in weakness." The word *flesh* is used in different ways in the Scripture. The vast majority of the time it is used to describe the innocent, created body. Hebrews 10:20 even uses the word flesh to describe the sinless body of Jesus. Yet sometimes it is used to describe the antithesis of spiritual things.

1. What is warring against the spirit in this verse?

   Galatians 5:17—For the flesh [lusts] against the Spirit, and the Spirit against the flesh: and these are contrary the one to the other: so that [you] cannot do the things that [you] would.

   _____

   What is warring against our ability to do right?

   *Romans 7:20–23—Now if I do that I would not, it is no more I that do it, but sin that [dwells] in me. I find then a law, that, when I would do good, evil is present with me. For I delight in the law of God after the inward man: but I see another law in my members, warring against the law of my mind, and bringing me into captivity to **the law of sin** which is **in my members**.*

   _____

   According to this passage where is the law or principle of indwelling sin?

   _____

   _____

Not only is our innocent, created body indwelt by a principle of sin, but when we give in to the impulse of that indwelling influence, we imprint ourselves with a lasting pattern of sinful behavior. Imagine that "doing right" is a straight and narrow path on the top of a ridge, and sin as a village down in the valley below. Each time we sin we engrave more and more well-worn paths away from God's straight and narrow way, making it easier and easier to sin and harder and harder not to.

2. The new spirit God has created in us is willing to do right, but what is weak?

   Matthew 26:41—Watch and pray, that [you] enter not into temptation: the spirit indeed is willing, **but the flesh is weak.**

   _____

Romans 8:3 teaches us that the flesh is weak and cannot live up to God's standards. The picture painted of our flesh is clear. Though it was created innocent and is not sinful in itself, it is indwelt by sin, has been patterned by our sinful behavior, and is not able without God's intervention to meet God's expectations. **The flesh at its worst leads us away from God and the flesh at its best cannot please God.** As children we developed most of our coping mechanisms for life leaning on our human abilities. And even in our adult years when we don't get our way, we often try to control and manipulate our environment or the people around us to create what we feel we need. All humans whether saved or unsaved can improve the flesh, but that is not spiritual living. What God has promised Christians is the gift of "victory through our Lord Jesus Christ" (I Corinthians 15:57).

THE REALIZATION OF THE PROBLEM

Many ask the question "If God really is powerful and has given me power over sin, why am I not experiencing this power to overcome my temptations?" Let's look at a few verses that get to the root of the problem.

3. Is God unable to hear our cries for help and "save us" from ourselves?

   Isaiah 59:1–2—Behold, the Lord's hand is not shortened, that it cannot save; neither his ear heavy, that it cannot hear: but **your iniquities [sins] have separated** *between you and your God, and* **your sins have hid** *his face from you, that he will not hear.*

   _____

   What is the problem?

   _____

4. What kind of sin causes the Lord not to hear us when we pray?

   Psalm 66:18—If I **regard iniquity [sin]** *in my heart, the Lord will not hear me.*

   _____

Though there is much more about this topic to be discussed, God cannot be compartmentalized. He is not going to give us victory in one area of our lives while we rebel against Him in another area. We must understand that harboring known sin in any area of our lives causes God to see us as resisting Him. Therefore, we are not available to receive His enabling strength.

5. The word *world* also has different meanings in various places throughout the Bible. What does it mean in this verse?

    *1 John 2:16—For all that is in the world, **the lust of the flesh**, and **the lust of the eyes**, and **the pride of life**, is not of the Father, but is of the world.*

    _____

6. What does God call us when we try to maintain our relationship with the lust of the flesh, the lust of the eyes, and the pride of life?

    *James 4:4—[Don't you know] that the friendship of the world is **enmity with God**? Whosoever therefore will be a friend of the world is the **enemy of God**.*

    _____

Romans 8:7 teaches us why this is true. "Because the carnal [fleshly] mind is enmity against God: for it is not subject to the law of God, neither indeed can be." Let's look at the harm and futility of trying to live out of the resources of our flesh.

THE PROBLEM OF GIVING IN TO THE SINS OF THE FLESH

In 1 John 2:16 we saw three areas in which the flesh can cause us to sin and separate us from the power of God.

THE SENSUAL SINS OF THE FLESH: THE LUST OF THE FLESH

7. God tells us that since we are believers it is incongruous for us to participate in the sensual sins in which many in our world participate. How does this type of sin affect us now that we are joined to Christ in salvation?

    *1 Corinthians 6:13–18—Now the body is not for fornication [physical intimacy outside of marriage], but for the Lord. . . . Know [you] not that your bodies are the members of Christ? shall I then take the members of Christ, and make them the members of an harlot? God forbid. What? know [you] not that he which is joined to an harlot is one body? for two, [says] he, shall be one flesh. But he that is joined unto the Lord is one spirit. **Flee fornication**. Every sin that a man [does] is without the body; but he that [commits] fornication [sins] **against his own body**.*

    What are we to do about it?

    _____

In Matthew 5:28 Jesus Himself told His followers not to even "look on a woman to lust after her" because ***it produces a deadening effect on the spiritual life of the inner man.*** Romans 8:13 teaches, "If [you] live after the flesh, [you] shall die." Death, in this case, is separation from God. Now clearly it is not the loss of eternal salvation, but it does take away that close relationship with God that gives us the zeal, desire, and ability to please Him. Sensual sins of the flesh come in many different forms, for example, pornography, binge eating, drunkenness, and illicit drug use.

THE MATERIALISTIC SINS OF THE FLESH: THE LUST OF THE EYES

8. Does the Bible say it is wrong to be rich? What does it say is wrong?

   *1 Timothy 6:9–10—But they that **will be** rich fall into temptation and a snare, and into many foolish and hurtful lusts, which drown men in destruction and perdition. For **the love of money** is the root of all [kinds of] evil: which while some coveted after, they have erred from the faith, and pierced themselves through with many sorrows.*

   _____

9. Who does God command Christians to avoid?

   1 Corinthians 5:11—I have written unto you not to keep company, if any man that is called a brother be a fornicator, or covetous, or an idolater, or a railer [someone using abusive language], or a drunkard, or an extortioner.

   _____

   Which of these sins seems less damaging to you? What does God say about it?

   Ephesians 5:3—But fornication, and all uncleanness, or covetousness, let it not be once named among you, as [becomes] saints.

   _____

The word *covetous* literally means "hungry for more." The idea is craving for what God has chosen not to give you. We will investigate this more in lesson 11, but this prevalent sin in the American culture is another deadening influence on the spiritual life of the inner man. Note: With each of these sin categories, the most destructive problem is the progressive nature of sin. Romans 6:19 teaches that when we "yield" ourselves to sin, that sin has an energy of its own, which moves us deeper into sin.

Materialistic sins of the flesh come in many different forms; for example, living outside our means, excessive debt, not being content with what we have.

THE SOCIAL SINS OF THE FLESH: THE PRIDE OF LIFE

The "social" sins are so called because they affect our relationships with others. Some of these manifestations of pride are being quick to anger, snipping at people with our words, manipulating or trying to control others, looking down on those who are different than we are, talking about people behind their backs, refusing to forgive, and bitterness.

10. It may appear that these are "little sins" compared to some we have looked at, but what does the Bible say about the sin of bitterness (unforgiveness)?

    *Hebrews 12:15–16—Looking diligently lest any man fail of the grace of God; lest any root of bitterness springing up trouble you, **and thereby many be defiled**; lest there be any fornicator, or profane person.*

    _____

Lesson 1 gave a description in Romans 3 of the nature of man. Romans is a book that deals with man's nature and God's provision of righteousness to correct the problem of sin in our lives. Romans 1–3 shows us the wickedness of our flesh. Romans 4–5 shows us the provision of Christ for our forgiveness and justification. Romans 6–8 shows us the continuing work of salvation through the provision of Christ for our sanctification. The word *sanctify* and the phrase *make holy* are essentially the same.

Now that you are a believer, God wants you to live like Him. In fact, 1 Peter 1:16 teaches us to "be . . . holy; for I [God] am holy."

Romans 1–3 shows how bad man is so that when we get to Romans 4–5 we realize God does all the saving and we can do nothing to help ourselves but trust in His gracious provision.

Romans 6 shows us that God's provision for salvation includes a present "saving from the power of sin." Before He shows us in Romans 8 how to effectively utilize His ongoing work of salvation, He again shows us the inability of self (our flesh) to overcome the indwelling law of sin residing in our flesh. He shows us that in sanctification as well as in salvation He does all the saving.

Though we must participate with God's gracious provision by steps of obedience, we can do nothing without Him. Jesus said, "without me [you] can do nothing" (John 15:5).

An understanding of Romans 7 gives us an idea of how powerless our flesh is to conform to God's holy standard, which was perfectly manifested in Christ's life.

11. Answer the following questions after reading the following passage from Scripture.

   *Romans 7:18–24—For I know that in me (that is, in my flesh,) **[dwells] no good thing:** for to will is present with me; but how to perform that which is good I find not. For the good that I would [want to do] I do not: but the evil which I would not [don't want to do], that I do. Now if I do that I would not [don't want to do], it is no more I that do it, but sin that [dwells] in me. I find then a law, that, when I would [want to] do good, evil is present with me. For I delight in the law of God after the inward man: but I see another law in my members, warring against the law of my mind, and bringing me into captivity to the law of sin which is in my members. O wretched man that I am! who shall deliver me from the body of this death?*

   Does anything good reside in our flesh?

   _____

   Can the flesh help me do what is right before God?

   *but **how to perform that which is good I find not.***

   _____

   What dwells in me that causes me to consistently do wrong?

   *but **sin that [dwells] in me.** I find then a law, that, when I would [want to] do good, evil is present with me. For I delight in the law of God after the inward man: but I see another law in my members, warring against the law of my mind, and bringing me into captivity to **the law of sin which is in my members.***

   _____

   What is the law of indwelling sin?

   _____

What are some good things you think you should be doing?

_____

What keeps you from doing those things?

_____

The law of indwelling sin is like the law of gravity. Gravity is the constant pull toward the center of the earth. It is a law that can never be broken, though it can be overcome by a stronger law. The law of indwelling sin is the constant pull within each man to sin. This principle dwells in every man and cannot be broken or outgrown as long as we live here on earth.

No wonder Paul cries out in such anguish! However, the next verse does let us know there is hope: "I thank God through Jesus Christ our Lord. So then with the mind I myself serve the law of God; but with the flesh the law of sin" (Romans 7:25).

The law of aerodynamics is the upward lift created as air flows over the upper and lower surfaces of a wing at differing speeds, thus allowing a winged aircraft to overcome the law of gravity when it achieves sufficient speeds. Just as gravity can be overcome by the law of aerodynamics, the law of indwelling sin can be overcome by the law of righteousness found in Jesus Christ. It is important to understand, that the weakness of the flesh leads to sin, and that leaning on the strength of human energy (flesh) cannot produce anything better.

THE PROBLEM OF ATTEMPTING TO LIVE THE CHRISTIAN LIFE IN OUR OWN STRENGTH

We know that the flesh is not strong enough to give us salvation. Even if a man tries with all his might to be good enough to get to heaven, he can never do it. Titus 3:5 teaches that it is "not by works of righteousness which we have done, but according to his mercy he saved us." However, many people have come to believe that the road to sanctification (becoming holy in thought and deed) is earned through self-effort (Galatians 3:2–3).

THE FLESH CAN'T PRODUCE SPIRITUAL LIVING

12. Can the flesh be profitable for sanctification?

Romans 8:5–8—For they

that are after the flesh do mind the things of the flesh;

but they that are after the Spirit the things of the Spirit.

For to be carnally [fleshly] minded is death;

but to be spiritually minded is life and peace. Because

the carnal mind is enmity against God: for it is not subject to the law of God, neither indeed can be.

So then **_they that are in the flesh cannot please God._**

13. What does God say about the man who depends on his self-efforts of human energy?

*Jeremiah 17:5—Thus [says] the Lord; **Cursed [is] the man that [trusts] in man**, and [makes] flesh his arm [strength or confidence].*

_____

14. What is going to happen to the Christian's works that are done through self-dependence?

*1 Corinthians 3:11–15—For other foundation can no man lay than that is laid, which is Jesus Christ. Now if any man build upon this foundation gold, silver, precious stones, **wood, hay, stubble**; every man's work shall be made manifest [shown for what it is]: for the day shall declare it, because it **shall be revealed by fire**; and the fire shall try every man's work of what sort it is. If any man's work abide which he has built thereupon, he shall receive a reward. If any man's **work shall be burned**, he shall suffer loss: but he himself shall be saved; yet so as by fire.*

_____

EVEN TRYING TO DO GOOD WHILE LIVING OUT OF THE RESOURCES OF THE FLESH IS COUNTERPRODUCTIVE

15. What does the Bible say about Bible-based teaching done in dependence on the flesh?

*2 Corinthians 3:6—For the **letter [kills]**, but the spirit [gives] life.*

_____

In the context of the passage, "letter" refers to truth apart from the effective work of the Holy Spirit. Even Bible preaching can be done in the energy of the flesh, and this passage teaches that kind of ministry is counterproductive.

How many parents have tried to correct their child (a good thing) out of the energies of their own flesh and ended up with a "will against will" argument that hurt the situation rather than helped. God didn't design us to live independently of Him, and when we try to do so, it will always create problems. (A good book on the subject is the *War of Words* by Paul David Tripp.)

DEPENDING ON OUR OWN ABILITIES APART FROM GOD IS SIN

16. What does the Bible call anything that is not done in dependence on the Lord?

*Romans 14:23—Whatsoever is not of faith is **sin**.*

_____

God never intended for man to live independently of Him. Before you were saved, everything you did was in your own strength and apart from Him. No wonder Proverbs 21:4 teaches us that even "the plowing of the wicked, is sin."

THE REASON FOR THIS DILEMMA

17.   Why would God leave us in such frail human bodies?

2 Corinthians 4:7—But we have this treasure in earthen vessels, **that the excellency of the power may be of God, and not of us**.

_____

Just three verses later 2 Corinthians 4:10 teaches that "the life also of Jesus might be made manifest in our body." Ephesians 3 likewise teaches that God's eternal purpose for man is to demonstrate the character of God through our lives while here on the earth. Through Christ's exchange this is now possible by the indwelling Spirit of Christ – "Christ in you the hope of glory" (Colossians 1:27).

APPLICATION

James 1:22–25 promises God's special blessing on those who take action on what His Word teaches.

In this lesson you have seen that sin is damaging to the Christian life and there is no ability to overcome its overwhelming control by our own self-efforts. Our only hope is the answer found in the Lord. We will look at the details concerning His provision in the next several lessons. Your need today is to admit the inability of your flesh and determine to look to God as your only source of victory. Will you do this today?

In the space below write your resolve in the form of a prayer.

_____

_____

_____

_____

_____

ASSIGNMENTS

Bible Reading: Matthew 1–7

Scripture Memory:

Matthew 26:41—Watch and pray, that [you] enter not into temptation: the spirit indeed is willing, but the flesh is weak.

(This verse is part of *The Exchange* Scripture Memory System.)

Practical Assignment: Has God shown you areas in which sin has dominion in your life? List these areas in the space below:

Sensual Sins

_____

Materialistic Sins

_____

Social Sins

_____

Doing good through human energy

_____

How is the Lord leading you to pray about these problems?

_____

_____

_____

_____

_____

_____

_____

LESSON 5

THE FULLNESS OF MY SAVIOR

UNDERSTANDING THE PROMISE OF CHRIST'S LIFE IN ME

We have already seen that we will never escape the negative pull of the flesh in this lifetime. It is like the constant pull of gravity. No matter how hard we *try*, we will never outgrow its effects. Although there is nothing we can do to make the flesh better, the Lord has promised victory in this lifetime. This lesson will focus on those promises, studying the reality of His provision.

THE PROMISE OF VICTORY

1. What does God always provide?

   *2 Corinthians 2:14—Now thanks be unto God, which **always causes us to triumph** [literally, puts victory on parade in us] **in Christ**, and makes manifest [clearly sensed] the savour [fragrance] of His knowledge by us in every place.*

   _____

   In Whom?

   _____

2. What kind of life did Christ promise those who follow Him?

   *John 10:10—I am come that they might have **life**, and that they might have it more **abundantly**.*

   _____

3. What kind of work did Christ promise those that believe on Him?

   *John 14:12—Verily, verily [truly, truly], I say unto you, He that [believes] on me, the works that I do shall he do also; and **greater works than these shall he do**; because I go unto my Father.*

   _____

Why?

because ***I go unto my Father.***

_____

4. How much fruit does Jesus promise to those who abide in Him?

    *John 15:5—I am the vine, [you] are the branches: he that [abides] in me, and I in him, the same **[brings] forth** **much fruit**: for without me [you] can do nothing.*

_____

5. How much victory over fleshly desires does God promise when we walk in the Spirit?

    *Galatians 5:16—This I say then, Walk in the Spirit, and **[you] shall not fulfil the lust** [desires] **of the flesh**.*

_____

6. Is Christ able to keep you from falling back into sin?

    *Jude 1:24–25—Now unto him that is able **to keep you from falling**, and to present you faultless . . . both now and ever.*

_____

7. What has God done for us?

    *Colossians 1:13—Who **[has] delivered us** from the power of darkness, and **[has] translated us** into the kingdom of his dear Son.*

_____

8. Who gives us both the desire and ability to do the things that please God—God or self?

    *Philippians 2:13—For **it is God which [works] in you both to will and to do** of his good pleasure.*

_____

All these promises of victory over sin and power for ministry do not remove the tendency to do wrong from the Christian. Remember in lesson 4 that we discovered the law of sin still resides in the believer and has a tendency to keep us from doing what is right, even when we want to do right (Romans 7:18–24). Jesus does not promise to remove the influences of the flesh and the world, He but gives us strength to overcome them. For example, a person with myopia will have trouble seeing things at a distance, but corrective lenses counteract the problem. The problem is not removed; but as long as his lenses are in place, he can see as well as if he didn't have myopia. He must choose to depend on the glasses before they will help him. As soon as he takes off his glasses, he will revert to his former way of seeing. In a similar manner, Romans 13:14 teaches us to "put . . . on the Lord Jesus Christ, and make not provision for the flesh, to fulfil the lusts thereof." As long as we depend on Him, He gives us the ability to refuse the desires of our flesh, though we may still feel them.

THE PERSON OF VICTORY

9. Who gives us the ability to overcome the influences of the world that tend to pull us away from God?

   1 John 4:4—[You] are of God, little children, and have overcome them: because greater is he that is in you, than he that is in the world.

   _____

   What does this verse say about your ability to live victoriously?

   Romans 8:37—In all these things we are more than conquerors through him that loved us.

   _____

The root word used to translate both "overcome" and "more than conquerors" is the Greek word *nike*. It means "to prevail or to gain the victory."

10. In a spiritual sense, where and what is Christ today?

    *Colossians 1:27—To whom God would make known what is the riches of the glory of this mystery among the Gentiles; **which is Christ in you**, the **hope of glory**.*

    _____

11. Who is still alive and living His life though us?

    *Galatians 2:20—I am crucified with Christ: nevertheless I live; **yet not I, but Christ [lives] in me**: and the life which I now live in the flesh I live by the faith of the Son of God, who loved me, and gave himself for me.*

    _____

Paul writes that he died with Christ on the cross, but he was, nonetheless, still alive. His explanation of this paradox was that the life he was living on earth was actually Christ living His life through Paul. Hudson Taylor was the founder of the China Inland Mission. His life touched thousands in China and his ministry is still impacting millions in Asia today. He called this "not I, but Christ [lives] in me" principle the exchanged life.

12. How does one live this exchanged life?

    *And the life which I now live in the flesh I live **by the faith** of the Son of God, who loved me, and gave himself for me.*

    _____

The "exchanged life" shown in this verse is the ongoing work of the exchange we made with Christ at salvation. He traded places with us, taking our sins on Himself on the cross, and making us "the righteousness of God in him" (2 Corinthians 5:21). Our regenerated spirit has been recreated after God "in righteousness and true holiness" (Ephesians 4:24). This new nature is the lasting result of that exchange and is a gift, not something we get by working for it. In Galatians 3:1–3 Paul chides the Christians in Galatia for struggling to live their lives for Christ in the flesh after receiving salvation as a gift through grace. Christ wants to give us the power of His life, but we must choose to live dependent on Him for it ("by the faith of the Son of God"). You may be struggling to get rid of a sin that seems to be overwhelming you, and Paul taught, **"yet not I, but Christ lives in me."** It is Christ's life lived out in the believer who is choosing to depend on Him. Paul made it clear that he, Paul, was the one who was living, yet it is Christ who was living in him. A plain piece of iron can illustrate this. It is cold, dull black, and unbending. If that same piece of iron is put into the blacksmith's fire, it becomes hot, glowing red, and malleable. We can say that the fire is in the iron and has changed its characteristics though it would still have the tendency to return to its former state as soon as it is removed from the fire. Christ is the fire; we are the cold, dull, unbending iron. What is seen in the iron is not the iron-life but the fire-life. What is seen in the Spirit-filled Christian is not the self-life but the Christ-life.

A biblical illustration of this same truth is found in John 15 where Jesus makes an analogy of the Christian life. He is the vine and we are the branches. We can produce fruit only as we abide in Him. We do not have the innate ability to bear fruit, but He does. We produce fruit by abiding in Him. Just like the sap from the vine produces fruit through the branch, it is the life of Christ that produces fruit in us. When we abide in Christ, we are living the Christ-life.

13. What does Christ offer to those who attach themselves to Him through belief?

   *John 7:38–39—He that [believes] on me, as the scripture [has] said, **out of his belly** [inner man] **shall flow** rivers of living water. (But this [spoke] he of **the Spirit**.)*

   _____

14. What does the Son give to those who live in Him?

   *John 8:36—If the **Son** therefore shall make you free, [you] **shall be free** indeed.*

   _____

15. From what does Jesus deliver us?

   *Galatians 1:4—Who [Jesus] gave himself for our sins, that he might deliver us from **this present evil world**, according to the will of God and our Father*

   _____

16. Whose life is clearly seen in the life of one who chooses to identify with the death of Christ through death to self?

   *2 Corinthians 4:10—Always bearing about in the body the dying of the Lord Jesus, that **the life also of Jesus** might be made manifest in our body.*

   _____

The word *manifest* is an interesting word that appears often in the Bible. It is not just being Christlike. It is showing Christ's life through yours. A good illustration of this is a room that has an inherent tendency to be dark. Imagine a room without any windows or doors. It has no ability in its own nature to be light. The characteristic of the room is darkness. Now place a bright light in the center of that room. Immediately the characteristic of the room is changed from darkness to light. The room itself does not change. If the light were to be turned out (stopped being depended upon), the characteristic of the room would once again plunge into darkness. Our life has the awful characteristics of darkness with no ability to have light, but Jesus is light. When we place Him at the center of our life, He changes the characteristics of our life from those of darkness to those of light. Not only have we become more Christlike but Christ's life is shining through us. This is what it means to have the life of Jesus made manifest in our body.

So how do we do this? The answer is simple faith. "Therefore being justified **by faith**, we have peace with God through our Lord Jesus Christ: **by whom also** we have access **by faith** into this grace wherein we stand, and rejoice in hope of the glory of God" (Romans 5:1–2). Faith that accesses justification has three essential elements: understanding, agreeing, and depending (This information is expanded in *The Exchange: An Inquirer's Bible Study*, available at www.exchangemessage.org.) Faith that accesses the **"grace wherein we stand"** has those same three essential elements though they may be expressed somewhat differently because now we are trusting God for a change of practice and not a positional change.

THE PURSUIT OF VICTORY

APPREHEND (UNDERSTAND) THE TRUTH

17. Circle the key words *know* or *knowing* in the following passage.

*Romans 6:3–10—Know [you] not, that so many of us as were baptized ª[**placed** into, or immersed] **into Jesus Christ** were baptized [placed] into his death? Therefore we are buried with him by baptism [immersion] into death: that like as Christ was raised up from the dead by the glory of the Father, even so we also should walk in newness of life. For if we have been planted together in the likeness of his death, we shall be also in the likeness of his resurrection: knowing this, that ᵇ**our old man** [unregenerate spirit] **is crucified with him**, that the body of sin [manifestation of sin] might be destroyed [rendered inoperative], that henceforth we should not serve sin. For he that is dead is freed from sin. Now if we be dead with Christ, we believe that ᶜ**we shall also live with him**: knowing that Christ being raised from the dead [dies] no more; death [has] no more dominion over him. For in that he died, he died unto sin once: but in that he [lives], he [lives] unto God.*

What are the three things we are supposed to know?

a.

_____

b.

_____

c.

_____

When we were placed into Christ at salvation, we were placed into His death and resurrection. At that moment our old man, or unregenerate spirit was crucified with Christ with the result that the body of sin, or the manifestation of sin in our lives, can now be rendered inoperative, and we are free from the slavery of sin. We have been made alive in the resurrection of Christ, which gave Him permanent power over death and sin and the ability to live pleasing to God.

Living under the tyranny of sin is likened to slavery. Can you imagine yourself as a slave under a tyrannical master? Imagine the forced labor, bad treatment, and horrible living conditions. Now imagine yourself purchased at great price and set free (redeemed) by a loving, kind, and generous landowner who lives across the road. He invites you to live with him and work for him. He has excellent living conditions, marvelous wages, and an affable personality that makes working for him a delight. This is the reality of what Jesus has done for you. The only difference is that not only were you bought by Him but you died to the mastery of sin by participating in His death on the cross and have been given the very life of Christ by participating in His resurrection. Sin's power over you has been rendered inoperative. Your old master still lives across the street so to speak and often calls out to you with demands to do his bidding. You still have the ability to walk back to those squalid conditions and give him your labors, but you don't have to anymore. Sin has no right to you! You are now free to live for your new master, Who, by the way, will reward you handsomely!

AGREE WITH THE TRUTH (RECKON THOSE THINGS TO BE TRUE ABOUT YOURSELF)

18. Circle the key word *reckon*.

> *Romans 6:11—Likewise reckon [you] also yourselves to be* ^a**dead indeed unto sin**, *but* ^b**alive unto God** *through Jesus Christ our Lord.*

The word *reckon* is an accounting term. It represents the same Greek word translated "imputed" several times in Romans 4. Just like God counts our faith for righteousness, we are to count what happened to Jesus as having happened to us.

> The idea is that you personally consider the truths concerning the crucifixion and resurrection of Christ to be true about yourself now that you have made the exchange with Him at salvation. What two things are you to consider to be true about yourself?

a.

_____

b.

_____

You are dead to sin and do not have to sin anymore. You are alive unto God and have the ability to live pleasing to Him. The day you were saved Christ accomplished in you what you could never have done for yourself. He did not die symbolically in your place. He died literally in your place! You received the full benefit of all that Christ did; and all that Christ is, **He** is in you.

As a result of this exchange, your old man, or unregenerate spirit that kept you from being able to relate to God, is gone. It died with Christ on the cross. In its place is a new regenerated spirit that is perfectly related to God through the resurrection power of Jesus. This new birth did not affect the flesh or the law of sin in your members, which are still vying for control of your actions. It did, however, open the way for you to relate to God openly, without any hesitation. "Let us therefore come boldly unto the throne of grace" (Hebrews 4:16). You are a new person. "If any man be in Christ, he is a new creature: old things are passed away; behold, all things are become new" (2 Corinthians 5:17). You now have the ability to live obediently as Jesus produces genuine godly living through your life. You can choose to continue on in sin if you desire, but you have the power through your participation in the crucifixion and resurrection of Christ to live apart from sin and pleasing to God.

APPROPRIATE THE TRUTH (ACT IN ACCORDANCE WITH AND BY THE POWER OF THE TRUTH)

In his book *The Great Exchange* Jerry Bridges makes this statement: "As we continue in union with Christ, transforming power is provided as we depend on the Holy Spirit's enablement in our ongoing battle against sin's presence in our lives."

19. Circle the key word *yield* in the following passage.

> *Romans 6:12–19—[Don't allow] sin therefore reign in your mortal [temporal] body, that you should obey it in the lusts thereof.* **Neither yield [you] your members as instruments of unrighteousness unto sin**: *but yield yourselves*

unto God, as those that are alive from the dead, and your members as instruments of righteousness unto God. For sin shall not have dominion over you: for [you] are not under the law, but under grace. What then? shall we sin, because we are not under the law, but under grace? God forbid. Know [you] not, that to whom [you] yield yourselves servants to obey, his servants [you] are to whom [you] obey; whether of sin unto death, or of obedience unto righteousness? But God be thanked, that [you] were the servants of sin, but [you] have obeyed from the heart that form of doctrine which was delivered you [you chose to depend upon the gospel message]. Being then made free from sin, [you] became the servants of righteousness. I speak after the manner of men because of the infirmity of your flesh: for as [you] have yielded your members servants to uncleanness and to iniquity unto iniquity; even so now yield your members servants to righteousness unto holiness.

I am not supposed to yield my members to _____

I am supposed to yield my members to _____

*but **yield yourselves unto God**, as those that are alive from the dead, and your members as instruments of righteousness unto God.*

What enables you to have victory over sin now that you are a Christian?

*for **[you] are** not under the law, but **under grace.***

_____

Paul uses an analogy that we all understand because we all have to live with the weakness of our own flesh. Have you ever been in a conversation in which you meant only to share a small tidbit of gossip and you ended up saying a whole lot more than you intended? Have you ever decided to take a peek at something you knew you shouldn't look at and ended up watching the whole thing, or looking at the whole magazine, and so forth? Paul teaches us that just as sin carries us along in an ebb of seemingly irresistible current once we choose to yield to its influence, even so grace carries the Christian along who chooses to yield to the Holy Spirit's influence in dependent obedience.

Knowing that Jesus has already won the victory over sin and death, your assuming that it is available to you and stepping out on those facts through steps of obedience is the essence of faith. Faith is like a switch in an electric fan. When a fan has access to electricity in the wall, the motor draws on the power of that electricity when the switch is turned on. In the spiritual realm grace is the energy that enables the "instrument" to function in power.

APPLICATION

James 1:22–25 promises God's special blessing to those who take action on what His Word teaches.

In this lesson you have seen that God has promised us victory over sin through our relationship with the crucified and risen Savior. Your job is not to work up the willpower to overcome sin. Your job is (1) to understand your participation with Christ in His death and resurrection broke the power of sin and is the foundation for your victory over sin, (2) consider that victory already yours personally, then (3) begin making choices to depend on that reality by simply choosing to stop doing wrong and start doing right. You have the power as part of the inheritance you received in salvation. Will you choose to start depending on that power and step out in its victory today?

Write your resolve in the form of a prayer.

_____

_____

_____

_____

_____

_____

_____

ASSIGNMENTS

Bible Reading: Matthew 8–14

Scripture Memory:

John 10:10—The thief [comes] not, but for to steal, and to kill, and to destroy: I am come that they might have life, and that they might have it more abundantly.

(This verse is part of *The Exchange* Scripture Memory System.)

Practical Assignment: Explain what the Christ-life is.

_____

_____

_____

_____

_____

_____

_____

LESSON 6

THE FOUNTAIN OF MY SURRENDER

APPROPRIATING THE POWER OF GOD IN MY LIFE

From lesson 1 we learned that God was grieved because His people had forsaken Him, "the fountain of living waters." If we are to experience His promised victory over sin, we must "draw water out of the wells of salvation." God has given us a vast inheritance, but He has given us the human responsibility to "write the checks," or make withdrawals through steps of faith. From lesson 4 we learned that sin is the problem, and we cannot expect any help from the flesh. In the last lesson we learned that Jesus is the answer and has provided overcoming power through His life in us. This lesson will show the key that unlocks God's power for living: the surrender of our will to God's will. Had Jesus not prayed, "Not my will, but thine, be done," and surrendered to the Father's will, He would never have gone to the cross and would never have experienced God's resurrection power.

John Paton was a missionary among the cannibals of the New Hebrides. In November of 1866 John and his family moved to the small island of Aniwa. Because the highest point was only three hundred feet above sea level, rain clouds did not regularly form over the island. The heavy dew from the humid climate made the island lush, and food was abundant. However, there was often a shortage of drinking water because there was no natural source of water, and the porous nature of the land made water storage difficult. When John decided to dig a well, the native people thought he was crazy. In all their years of living on the island, fresh water came only from the rain. John assured them that God had placed water in the ground, and he began digging to prove it. The water was there all the time; he only had to draw it out by uncovering it. At the depth of thirty feet he hit a spring of water that provided fresh water for the island for years.

In a similar way God has placed the rivers of living water in the inner man of every believer. God's purpose for each of us is to demonstrate His life to the world through His Spirit flowing out of our inner man, producing the fruit of righteousness in our lives. Sanctification is the process whereby God makes us progressively more holy like Himself. He does this by removing more and more of self through our surrender and revealing more and more of Himself.

1. What are the three elements of faith we learned about from Romans 6? (Feel free to look back at pages 44–46.)

    A _____ or *K* _____

    A _____ or *R* _____

    A _____ or *Y* _____

The words were *Apprehend,* or *Know—Agree with,* or *Reckon—Appropriate,* or *Yield.* Before a person can really *believe* something, all three of these elements must be present. One cannot *believe* something that he doesn't understand. Nor can he believe if he understands but doesn't personally agree. And most importantly he does not really believe in something until he actually begins to depend on it by taking steps of faith.

Missing this last element of actually yielding one's life to God causes many people to fail to draw precious water from the wells of salvation.

What do you think yield means in these verses?

Romans 6:19b; 22—Neither yield . . . your members as instruments of unrighteousness unto sin: but yield yourselves unto God, as those that are alive from the dead, and your members as instruments of righteousness unto God. . . . I speak after the manner of men because of the infirmity of your flesh: for as [you] have yielded your members servants to uncleanness and to iniquity unto iniquity; even so now yield your members servants to righteousness unto holiness. . . . But now being made free from sin, and become servants to God, [you] have your fruit unto holiness.

_____

_____

In this context the word *yield* means to present. You are not to present your body to sin, but you are to present your body to God. When we do this, we allow His fruit of holiness to flow through our lives. We must say **"no"** to the desires of our flesh and **"yes"** to God, surrendering to His will and depending on His power.

Jesus said it this way to His disciples, "If any man will come after me, let him deny himself, and take up his cross, and follow me" (Matthew 16:24). Before you can follow Jesus, you must deny yourself. Before we say "yes" to Jesus, we have to say "no" to self.

WE MUST DIE TO THE SELF-LIFE

SELF-LIFE—TRUSTING IN SELF AND LIVING FOR SELF

2. Read Romans 6:16 and 19 again. These verses teach a practical way believers draw on the righteousness of Jesus deposited in our "account" when He made the exchange with us at salvation.

*Romans 6:16, 19—Know [you] not, that to whom [you] **yield yourselves servants** to obey, his **servants** [you] are to whom [you] obey; whether of sin unto death, or of obedience unto righteousness? . . . I speak after the manner of men because of the infirmity of your flesh: for as **[you] have yielded** your members servants to uncleanness and to iniquity unto iniquity; **even so now yield** your members servants to righteousness unto holiness.*

What words in verse 16 indicate a necessary change in order to be able to obey God?

_____

We have been slaves to sin all our lives. What can we learn about sin's mastery over us that can teach us how to let righteousness rule in our lives?

_____

The picture of sin painted in its first mention in the Bible is of an animal crouching at the door of disobedience about to leap on its prey. God says that sin will have mastery over a man unless that man gains the mastery over it (Genesis 4:7).

Do you remember a time when you made a decision to do something wrong and sensed that there seemed to be an energy that swept you along in sin with hardly the ability to stop until the sin was done, for example, saying angry words, stepping into immorality, stealing something from a store? This passage teaches that the same kind of energy from God's Holy Spirit will carry you along to do something that God wants you to do once you "**yield,**" or "**present,**" yourself to Him for that task. **Stop trusting in your abilities and stop trying to please yourself.**

Paul first presented the truth about our victory in Christ in Romans 6. In chapter 7 he pointed out the inability of the flesh to fulfill the righteousness of the Law of God but ends the chapter with hope.

> *Romans 7:25—I thank God through Jesus Christ our Lord. So then with the mind I myself serve the law of God; but with the flesh the law of sin.*

Romans 8 restores our confidence that we can live for God in this lifetime.

3. We have already seen the continuing effect of the law of sin in a Christian's life, but what is the stronger law that gives us victory to overcome?

   Romans 8:2—For the law of the Spirit of life in Christ Jesus [has] made me free from the law of sin and death.

   _____

   Who can fulfill the righteousness of the law?

   *Romans 8:3-4—For what the law could not do, in that it was weak through the flesh, God sending his own Son in the likeness of sinful flesh, and for sin, condemned sin in the flesh: that **the righteousness of the law might be fulfilled in us, who walk not after the flesh, but after the Spirit.***

   _____

We can fulfill the righteousness of the law when we walk dependent on the Spirit, drawing from the resources of the Spirit of God.

4. What must we say no to before we can be spiritually minded?

   *Romans 8:5–7—For **they that are after the flesh do mind the things of the flesh;** but they that are after the Spirit the things of the Spirit. For **to be carnally [fleshly] minded is death;** but to be spiritually minded is life and peace. Because **the carnal mind is enmity against God:** for it is not subject to the law of God, neither indeed can be.*

   _____

Romans 8 continues, promising the progressive sanctification of each of God's true children culminating in the glorification of our bodies in Heaven.

What can separate us from the love of God?

Romans 8:35–39—Who shall separate us from the love of Christ? shall tribulation, or distress, or persecution, or famine, or nakedness, or peril, or sword? As it is written, For thy sake we are killed all the day long; we are accounted as sheep for the slaughter. Nay, in all these things we are more than conquerors through him that loved us. For I am persuaded, that neither death, nor life, nor angels, nor principalities, nor powers, nor things present, nor things to come, nor height, nor depth, nor any other creature, **shall be able to separate us from the love of God, which is in Christ Jesus our Lord.**

Paul interrupts his description of the ongoing work of salvation in the lives of God's true children by giving us a history lesson about the nation of Israel and their rejection of God's plan (Romans 9–11). He warns those of us who have become true children of God to continue on in God's goodness lest we be cut off from the blessings of God (Romans 11:17–22).

Paul then brings us back to the call to surrender that he began in Romans 6. The same word that is translated "yield" there is translated "present" in Romans 12:1.

5. Is God someone you can trust with your life?

   Romans 11:33–36—O the depth of the riches both of the wisdom and knowledge of God! how unsearchable are his judgments, and his ways past finding out! For who [has] known the mind of the Lord? or who [has] been his counsellor? Or who [has] first given to him, and it shall be recompensed unto him again? For **of him,** *and* **through him,** *and* **to him, are all things:** *to whom be glory for ever. Amen.*

He is an awesome God, Who is completely trustworthy. His steadfast love for you and His ability to care for you are unquestionable. We are commanded to present our bodies to God, but before that command is one of the most comprehensive statements of His greatness: "Of him, and through him, and to him, are all things." All men will present themselves to Him someday! Only when we present our earthly bodies to Him will we enjoy the benefits of giving Him glory in this lifetime.

6. What does God plead for you to do?

   Romans 12:1–2—I beseech you therefore, [brothers], by the **mercies of God,** *that [you]* **present your bodies a living sacrifice,** *holy, acceptable unto God, which is your reasonable service. And be not conformed to this world: but be . . . transformed by the renewing of your mind, that [you] may prove what is that good, and acceptable, and perfect, will of God.*

What gives a Christian the ability to present his body as a living sacrifice?

How would you describe a life that has been presented to God as a "living sacrifice"?

The word *sacrifice* may sound like simply giving something up, but to the world in which Paul was writing it could mean only one thing—death. Yet, it is called a "living sacrifice."

In Galatians 2:20 Paul wrote, "**I am crucified** with Christ: nevertheless **I live**; yet not I, but Christ [lives] in me." Do you see both death and life in this verse?

You learned from Romans 6 that when you were placed into Jesus the day you were saved, you were placed into His death. Dying to self is not a new activity on your part. You have been crucified with Christ. Dying to self is a choice to live in the reality of the exchange He made with you at salvation. It is part of "writing the checks" to the inheritance He gave us. It is real. Your old man died with Christ that day. You have been given His life. Now you must depend on that reality by making choices to say no to self and the flesh and to present your body to God for His use. Those choices will begin to bring change into your life.

What is our relationship to "this world" after we have presented our bodies as a living sacrifice to God?

And **be not conformed to this world**: but be . . . transformed.

7. What did Jesus teach was the cost of true discipleship?

*Matthew 10:37–39—He that [loves] father or mother more than me is not worthy of me: and he that [loves] son or daughter more than me is not worthy of me. And **he that [takes]** not **his cross**, and [follows] after me, is not worthy of me. He that [finds] his life shall lose it: and **he that [loses] his life** for my sake shall find it.*

*Matthew 16:24–26—Then said Jesus unto his disciples, If any man will come after me, let him **deny himself**, and **take up his cross**, and follow me. For whosoever will save his life shall lose it: and whosoever will **lose his life** for my sake shall find it. For what is a man profited, if he shall gain the whole world, and lose his own soul? Or what shall a man give in exchange for his soul?*

*Luke 9:57–62—And it came to pass, that, as they went in the way, a certain man said unto him, Lord, I will follow [You wherever You go]. And Jesus said unto him, foxes have holes, and birds of the air have nests; but the Son of man [has] not where to lay his head. And he said unto another, follow me. But he said, Lord, suffer [allow] me first to go and bury my father. Jesus said unto him, Let the dead bury their dead: but go . . . and preach the kingdom of God. And another also said, Lord, I will follow You]; but let **me first** go bid them farewell, which are at home at my house. And Jesus said unto him, **No man, having put his hand to the plough, and looking back, is fit for the kingdom of God.***

*Luke 14:27–33—And whosoever [does] not bear his cross, and come after me, cannot be my disciple. For which of you, intending to build a tower, [sits] not down first, and **[counts] the cost**, whether he has sufficient to finish it? Lest . . . after he [has] laid the foundation, and is not able to finish it, all that behold it begin to mock him, saying, This man began to build, and was not able to finish. Or what king, going to make war against another king, [sits] not down first, and **[consults] whether he is able** with ten thousand to meet him that [comes] against him with twenty thousand? Or else, while the other is yet a great way off, he [sends an ambassador], and [desires] conditions of peace. So likewise, whosoever he [is] of you that **[forsakes] not all that he [has]**, he cannot be my disciple.*

Some understand the surrender Jesus requires from His disciples at salvation, others come to it a little at a time, but many have a point in which they choose to surrender all to Jesus. **This surrender is** not a work but a decision. It is not deciding to do better or trying harder but **choosing to believe Him trustworthy and yielding every part of your life to His control**. You will find that even if you view surrender as total abandonment of yourself to God, it is not a onetime act, but must be repeated throughout your lifetime.

Amy Carmichael, a missionary who was greatly used of God, spent over forty years in India without a single trip home to her native England. The Lord used her not only to build several orphanages and save hundreds of children from wicked abuse in pagan temples but also to see longstanding immoral practices in India outlawed. She spoke of surrender this way: "In acceptance [lies] peace." It is accepting the fact that everything in my life that is out of my control is in His control and is given to me for my good.

> *Romans 8:28—And we know that all things work together for good to them that love God, to them who are the called according to his purpose.*

Surrender is yielding to His control all the areas about which we have a choice. It is not a passive surrender but an active giving of all that I am and all that I have to Him. To refuse to take this step of consecration is to live in suspicion of God's power and goodness. To take this step is to choose to depend on the fact that He is sovereign and He is good.

A song we often sing in church well summarizes this choice of your will. Will you read it carefully and consider making it your prayer of surrender?

> *All to Jesus I surrender,*
> *All to Him I freely give;*
> *I will ever love and trust Him,*
> *In His presence daily live.*
>
> *All to Jesus I surrender,*
> *Humbly at His feet I bow;*
> *Worldly pleasures all forsaken,*
> *Take me, Jesus, take me now.*
>
> *All to Jesus I surrender,*
> *Make me Savior wholly Thine;*
> *Let me feel the Holy Spirit,*
> *Truly know that Thou art mine.*
>
> *All to Jesus I surrender,*
> *Lord, I give myself to Thee;*
> *Fill me with Thy love and power,*
> *Let Thy blessing fall on me.*
>
> *I surrender all,*
> *I surrender all;*
> *All to Thee, my blessed Savior,*
> *I surrender all.*
>
> *Judson W. Van DeVenter*

WE MUST LIVE THE CHRIST-LIFE

BEING CONVINCED OF HIS VICTORY TO THE POINT OF ACTION

8. What kind of living sacrifice does God expect from us?

    *Romans 12:1–2—I beseech you therefore, [brothers], by the mercies of God, that [you] present your bodies a living sacrifice, **holy, acceptable unto God**, which is your reasonable service. And be not conformed to this world: but be . . . transformed by the renewing of your mind, that [you] may prove what is that **good, and acceptable, and perfect**, will of God.*

    _____

    Notice the verbs of command used in this passage.

    *Romans 12:1–2—I beseech you therefore, [brothers], by the mercies of God, that [you] **present your bodies** a living sacrifice, holy, acceptable unto God, which is your reasonable service. And **be not conformed** to this world: but **be . . . transformed** by the renewing of your mind, that [you] may prove what is that good, and acceptable, and perfect, will of God.*

All three main verbs are commands. The first verb is an active presentation of your body to the Lord. This is your responsibility, and it demands an active choice. If you want God to use your life, you must present it to Him. When you present your body to God, He takes it and uses it for His purposes. The next two verbs are passive and ongoing. "Be not conformed" means to stop being pressured into the mold of the world. (This concept will be discussed further in lesson 8.) The idea of "be transformed" is the progressive transformation into one who is showing the "good, and acceptable, and perfect, will of God." Notice this is passive. We can't be transformed through our flesh or our own willful choices. Our only hope for real change is found in God's abounding grace. We can have great confidence in the Christian's ability to change, but He must do the changing. Notice also, this is ongoing and you have the ongoing responsibility to remind yourself (the renewing of your mind) that you belong to Him. He will be faithful to progressively transform you into His image throughout the remainder of your earthly existence. Your part in this transformation is to remember who you belong to and renew your commitment to present your body to God with every decision you make. (We will discuss ways of doing this in lesson 7.)

The word *transform* means to be totally changed from the inside out. The English word *metamorphosis* comes from this word in the Greek language. The picture of a caterpillar spinning a cocoon and emerging as a butterfly establishes metamorphosis as a process that involves a radical change. The change the Bible paints of a Christian is even more radical. This unique Greek word is used only four times in the Bible. Twice it describes Christ, and twice it describes what Christ wants to do to His disciples.

When Jesus was here on earth, His deity was veiled by His human body. Toward the end of His earthly ministry He took three of His disciples to the top of a mountain.

9. In your own words describe what Jesus looked like.

    Matthew 17:2—And he was transfigured [transformed] before them: and his face did shine as the sun, and his raiment was white as the light.

    Mark 9:2–3—And after six days Jesus [took] with him Peter, and James, and John, and [led] them up into an high mountain apart by themselves: and he was transfigured before them. And his raiment became shining, exceeding white as snow; so as no fuller [launderer] on earth can white them.

For a moment Jesus pulled back the veil and allowed His disciples to see His deity. The Bible teaches He is **now** in you; and in the same way, He wants to show the world His nature through changing you.

10. With whom is God satisfied?

    *Matthew 3:17—And lo a voice from heaven, saying, This is **my beloved Son**, in whom I am well pleased.*

    *Matthew 17:5—While he yet [spoke], behold, a bright cloud overshadowed them: and behold a voice out of the cloud, which said, This is **my beloved Son**, in whom I am well pleased; hear . . . him.*

    _____

11. Describe how Christ's sacrifice impacted God the Father.

    *Ephesians 5:2—And walk in love, as Christ also [has] loved us, and [has] given himself for us an offering and a sacrifice to God for a **sweet smelling savour** [fragrance].*

    _____

12. In a similar way, how do we satisfy God?

    *2 Corinthians 2:15—For we are unto God a sweet savour [fragrance] **of Christ**.*

    _____

We will never be holy and acceptable to God through our own ability. This is why we must say no to *self*. Our acceptance comes from Christ and His transforming power. Do you ever feel there are things in your life you know are wrong but you can't seem to change them?

13. What does God promise you?

    *1 Corinthians 10:13—There [has] no temptation taken you but such as is common to man: but God is faithful, **who will not suffer [allow] you to be tempted above that [you] are able**; but will with the temptation also **make a way to escape, that [you] may be able to bear it**.*

    _____

    Would He tell you this if there were no real way of escape?

    _____

    Can you count on this promise for your life?

    _____

As a Christian you have grace through Christ to live victoriously before God. You may not always feel as though you have the strength, but remember Martin Luther's poem:

> *Feelings come and feelings go,*
> *And feelings are deceiving;*
> *My warrant is the Word of God*
> *Naught else is worth believing.*

In the exchange you made with Christ, you were given the power of the crucifixion and resurrection of Jesus, not the **feelings** of that power. **Your feelings are not a reliable source of truth.** You have the ability to choose to present your body to the power of Christ's victory or to yield to the feelings of defeat you may experience. Consider the following illustration: Imagine three men walking in a line. Mr. Fact knows which way, but Mr. Feeling doesn't feel right about the direction and wants to go another way. Mr. Faith is the one who must decide which direction to take. If he follows Mr. Feeling, they will leave Mr. Fact behind because he never changes. If Mr. Faith follows Mr. Fact, Mr. Feeling will come along behind—he never goes away. In fact, he will be complaining all along the way; but if Mr. Faith will hold firm and keep following Mr. Fact, eventually Mr. Feeling will change his mind, and they will all go along together happily—until Mr. Fact and Mr. Feeling disagree again.

I use a couplet to help me remember that I have the power to choose righteous living even when I don't **feel** righteous.

> *Act not on what you feel,*
> *But based on what is real!*

14. When is God's grace sufficient for you?

    *2 Corinthians 12:9—My grace **is** sufficient for [you]: for my strength is made perfect in weakness. Most gladly therefore will I rather glory in my infirmities, that the power of Christ may rest upon me.*

A preacher in the late 1800s struggled with the answer to this question. He had been on a holiday to the seashore. He tells the story, "My little daughter was taken sick and died. I had to carry the little coffin in my arms all the way home where I buried my little one with my own hands." He was to preach the next morning and settled on the text "My grace is sufficient for you."

He continues the story, "I sat down to prepare my notes, but soon found myself 'murmuring in my tent' against God for all He called upon me to bear. I flung down my pen, threw myself on my knees and said to God, 'It is not sufficient, it is not sufficient! Lord, let Your grace be sufficient. O Lord, do!'"

A beautifully illustrated Scripture text hung on the wall above his table. "As I opened my eyes I was saying, 'O God let Your grace be sufficient for me,' and there on the wall I saw 'MY GRACE IS SUFFICIENT FOR YOU.'

"The word 'is' was in bright green; 'my' was in black, and 'you' in black. 'MY grace **IS** sufficient for YOU.' I heard a voice that seemed to say to me, 'You fool, how dare you ask God to make what is! Get up and take, and you will find it true. When God says 'is' it is for you to believe Him and you will find it true at every moment.' That 'is' turned my life; from that moment I could say, 'O God, whatever [You did] say in Thy Word I believe, and . . . I will step out on it.'"

Will you step out on God's Word today? Go back and read the promises on page 48. They are true. You can count on them. You can step out on them. It is really a matter of submission to God. Do you trust Him enough to submit?

SUMMARY

Imagine that God has drawn a line in the sand of time and everyone on earth must stand on one side or the other. To the one side He promises to pour out the blessings of His grace and to the other the scorn of His opposition. Which side would you want to be on?

When we received Christ, we became sons of God. "But as many as received him, to them gave he power to become the sons of God, even to them that believe on his name" (John 1:12). Now that we are His children He is responsible for us. As a good father He is constantly at work in our lives. Therefore we cannot influence whether He spends energy on us, but we do determine what kind of energy He aims at us.

15. What kind of energy is God pouring out on man in each of these verses, and what provokes it?

Proverbs 3:34—Surely he [scorns] the scorners: but he [gives] grace unto the lowly.

_____

James 4:6—But he [gives] more grace. Wherefore he [says], **God [resists] the proud,** *but [gives] grace unto the* **humble**.

_____

1 Peter 5:5—Be clothed with humility: for God [resists] the proud, and [gives] grace to the humble.

_____

R*esist* is a military word that describes a long persistent siege on a city.

The story of Masada in southwest Israel is a dreadful illustration of a siege. The fortress of Masada was built between 37-31 BC and was all but abandoned by the time Jewish zealots fled there after the destruction of Jerusalem in AD 70. The Roman governor Flavius Silva laid siege to the fortress with the Tenth Legion in AD 73. They built camps at the base with a wall to prevent any of the more than the thousand men, women, and children on top of the mountain from escaping. Silva wanted to force the zealots to surrender. The construction of a rampart against the western gates of the fortress allowed a battering ram to breach the wall. According to the historian Josephus, all but two women, who escaped, committed suicide rather than surrender that last Jewish stronghold to the Romans.

Like the Roman governor, God wants those who proudly rebel against Him to surrender. Unlike the Roman governor, **God** doesn't want to conquer us but **wants to live an intimate relationship with us**. In James 4 He pleads with those walking in pride to draw near to Him in humble submission, and He promises to draw near to them with His provision of grace.

Pride, living as if we know better than God, keeps us from His grace. Isn't it time for you to surrender? Simply humble yourself before Him. **Yield** to all His claims on your life and **trust** all the promises in His Word. He "gives grace to the humble." The word *grace* is supernatural enabling from God to do His will. This enabling from God is real. You can count on it. Will you choose to step out on it today?

APPLICATION

James 1:22–25 promises God's special blessing to those who take action on what His Word teaches.

"The wells of salvation" are yours, yet many have forsaken "the fountains of living water" and through self-effort have built coping mechanisms of flesh. These "broken cisterns" cannot work and are a grief to God. He wants you to draw near to Him and "with joy . . . draw waters out of the wells of salvation" He has provided for us through the death of His own son. He is waiting for many to humble themselves so that He can pour His grace through their lives like "rivers of living water."

In this lesson you have seen that God expects us to step out on His Word and trust Him. Will you present yourself completely to Him today?

If your answer is yes, write your resolve in the form of a prayer. If your answer is no, write the areas of your life in which you are not willing to yield to Him and ask Him to make you willing to surrender.

_____

_____

_____

_____

_____

ASSIGNMENTS

Bible Reading: Matthew 15–21

Scripture Memory:

> *Romans 12:1–2—I beseech you therefore, brethren, by the mercies of God, that [you] present your bodies a living sacrifice, holy, acceptable unto God, which is your reasonable service. And be not conformed to this world: but be . . . transformed by the renewing of your mind, that [you] may prove what is that good, and acceptable, and perfect, will of God.*

(This verse is part of *The Exchange* Scripture Memory System.)

Practical Assignment: Describe the worst thing that has ever happened to you, for example, abusive situation, being lied about, being hurt in an accident, losing a loved one, being betrayed by someone you trusted.

_____

_____

_____

_____

_____

_____

In Genesis 50:20, Joseph, an Old Testament saint, was talking to his brothers about an abusive act they had committed against him when he was a boy. He said, "But as for you, [you] thought evil against me; but **God meant it unto good**, to bring to pass, as it is this day, to save much people alive." Can you look back on your situation and see anything that denotes the good hand of God in your circumstance? Record your thoughts.

_____

_____

_____

_____

_____

_____

First Thessalonians 5:18 says, "In every thing give thanks: for this is the will of God in Christ Jesus concerning you." Will you thank God for allowing this to happen to you? Write your resolve in the form of a prayer.

_____

_____

_____

_____

Is there someone in this situation you need to forgive or make restitution toward? What do you think God wants you to do about this?

_____

_____

_____

_____

_____

LESSON 7

THE FILLING OF MY SPIRIT

EXPERIENCING THE REALITIES OF GOD'S GRACE IN MY LIFE

The Old Testament records the story of Abraham's son Isaac moving his extensive herds to a valley that his father had lived in years before. When he got there, he discovered that an enemy army had filled in all of the wells his father had dug. In great need of water, he deployed all his servants to the task of finding and uncovering the wells. He was delighted to hear that not only had they accomplished the task but also that one of the wells was a natural spring water. He had been living right next to a fresh spring but didn't know it because it had been stopped up with rocks (Genesis 26:15-19).

We are all prone to allow the "rocks" of sin and self to stop up "the fountain of living waters" God placed in us at salvation.

If you've surrendered your life to Jesus, it was not a one-time act that made you "spiritual" from that point on.

To maintain the flow of the Holy Spirit through your life (John 7:38-39), you must refuse to allow the desires of the flesh to lodge in your heart. You must live a life committed to listening and surrendering to the voice of the Spirit. The Bible calls this the Spirit-filled life. Growth in the Spirit-filled life is the progressive peeling back of self so that more of Jesus is seen or more of the Spirit flows through you. As you learn more of God's nature, you grow in your understanding and experience. When you choose to apply each new lesson, and reckon each new truth about God to be true, He is seen more clearly. John the Baptist, who was the sent to prepare the way for Jesus, said it this way: "He must increase, but I must decrease" (John 3:30).

This lesson will investigate growing in grace, walking in the Spirit and enjoying a steady life of victory in Christ.

THE INDWELLING OF THE HOLY SPIRIT

1. Who is the Comforter Jesus promised to send to His disciples?

    *John 14:16–18—And I [Jesus] will pray the Father, and he shall give you **another** [One just like Me] **Comforter** [One who calls men alongside Himself], that he may abide [remain] with you for ever; even the **Spirit of truth**; whom the world cannot receive, because it [sees] him not, neither [knows] him: but you know him; for he [dwells] with you, and shall be in you. I will not leave you comfortless [orphaned]: I will come to you.*

Why can't an unbeliever have the Holy Spirit dwell in him or her?

_____

How did you come to know the Holy Spirit?

_____

We come to "know" the Holy Spirit by receiving Christ as our Savior.

How did Jesus plan to comfort His disciples?

_____

He has come to us through the person of the Holy Spirit.

2. Now that you "know" Him, where does He live?

    *1 Corinthians 6:19—What? Know [you] not that **your body is the temple of the Holy [Spirit]** which is in you, which [you] have of God, and [you] are not your own?*

    _____

Everyone that is born again has "passed from death to life" and is now "indwelt" by the Holy Spirit. That means that He lives in you, but it does not necessarily mean that you are "filled" with the Holy Spirit.

PICTURES OF SPIRIT-FILLED LIVING

3. To what does the Bible contrast being filled with the Holy Spirit?

    *Ephesians 5:18—And be not **drunk with wine**, wherein is excess; but be filled with the Spirit.*

    _____

What does a person have to do to be drunk with wine? He has to give himself liberally to the wine, and it begins to control all his thoughts and actions. It is as if he becomes another person. Note this is a command. God expects us to give the Holy Spirit control of our thoughts and actions. Then He begins to give us the grace to be what we could never be without Him. You may ask this question: Will I simply be a robot without my own personality and volition?

4. What analogy does the Lord use of the grace He gives to us regarding our speech?

    *Colossians 4:6—Let your speech be alway with grace, **seasoned with salt**, that [you] may know how [you] ought to answer every man.*

    _____

If a person puts salt on food, it enhances the taste and makes it more inviting to eat, but it does not change the nature of the food. In a similar way the Holy Spirit changes us, but we still retain the elements that make us the unique individual God created us to be. Another illustration might be the three human authors God used to write the Synoptic Gospels—Matthew, Mark, and Luke. The Scripture tells us that these men were controlled by the Holy Spirit, yet we clearly see the personality, viewpoint, and vocabulary of each individual author. The Holy Spirit's control over us causes us to be active, not passive. He does not bypass our own emotions, mind, and will. He brings each to the height of its capacity by supplying us with His supernatural ability.

5. In each of the following passages the result is exactly the same. What causes the result in each verse?

    *Ephesians 5:18–19—And be not drunk with wine, wherein is excess; but **be filled with the Spirit**; speaking to yourselves in psalms and hymns and spiritual songs, singing and making melody in your heart to the Lord.*

    _____

    *Colossians 3:16—**Let the word of Christ dwell in you richly in all wisdom**; teaching and admonishing one another in psalms and hymns and spiritual songs, singing with grace in your hearts to the Lord.*

    _____

Being filled with the Spirit of Christ and having the Word of Christ living luxuriously in a person is the same thing. This is more than simply filling our mind with God's Word. An unsaved professor of religion may know the Bible extremely well, even in the original languages, but that doesn't make him Spirit-filled. Spirit filling involves surrendering our will to God's. The word picture used is one of making Christ completely at home in our life. We can't tell Him that He's welcome into our living room but not our entertainment room. Just like alcohol controls all the thoughts and actions of a drunk man, we are to make Him feel at home in all the rooms in our "house."

There is a supernatural oneness between Christ and His Word in that He uses the Bible to progressively reveal more and more of Himself to us. Learning from Him, trusting in Him, and yielding to Him at every point is how to "grow in grace and in the knowledge of our Lord and Saviour Jesus Christ" (2 Peter 3:18). As we give Him free access to all the rooms of our life with each successive truth, promise, or command, we experience a greater sense of His presence and His power. It is similar to a close, growing human relationship. A husband and wife may have a superb relationship at the point of marriage; but as they grow to know each other better, only then can they adjust themselves to best fit their lives together. The main difference in our relationship with Jesus is that He never changes but is consistently, supernaturally changing us to fit our lives to Him more and more as we continue to surrender to Him.

It is important to note that if at any point along the way we rebel against Him through fear, unbelief, disobedience, pride, relying on our flesh, or a host of other sins, we hinder our growth. We have ceased to give the Holy Spirit control of our thoughts and actions and have ceased to be Spirit-filled by quenching His work in our lives.

6. This is not to say that the Spirit-filled life is a sinless life. What does the Bible say about the man who says he is perfect and without sin?

    *1 John 1:8—If we say that we have no sin, **we deceive ourselves**, and the truth is not in us.*

    _____

7. What kind of sin keeps a man from God's power?

    *Psalm 66:18—If I **regard iniquity in my heart**, the Lord will not hear me.*

    _____

God is patient with our ignorance. We will constantly be learning more about Him until the day we die. We will keep learning more of what He likes and what He doesn't like. As long as we are walking through life with Him and allowing Him to change us to fit with our growing understanding of Him, He will continue to give us His grace. Remember what causes God to resist a believer? ***Pride***.

> *James 4:6—God [resists] the proud, but [gives] grace unto the humble.*

Pride is thinking that we know better than God. When we say no to God and take our life off the altar of sacrifice, God will no longer bless us with His enabling grace. We will be stuck in a pattern of spiritual battle against God. God is true to His Word. He has promised to lay siege against our pride until we rid ourselves of our rebellion and humbly look to Him to reestablish His enabling grace in our lives.

8. How do we rid ourselves of the sin and unrighteousness of the self-life?

> *1 John 1:9—**If we confess our sins**, he is faithful and just to forgive us our sins, and to cleanse us from all unrighteousness.*

_____

9. What is the sign of insincere confession to God?

> *Proverbs 28:13—He that **[covers] his sins** shall not prosper: but [whoever confesses and **forsakes] them** shall have mercy.*

_____

What is the sign of genuine confession?

_____

The Spirit-filled life is part of the great inheritance we received the day we trusted Christ. To obtain the benefits of our Savior's provision, we must choose to live in surrender to Him and in reliance upon His promises. Then Christ lives His life of victory and power through ours because we are depending on Him to do so (Galatians 2:20). If we experience a victorious life through a decision of faith, then the growth of that life is not through self-efforts but through continuing in faith or walking by faith.

THE WALK OF FAITH

10. What will happen to us when we focus our attention on the glory of God?

> *2 Corinthians 3:18—But **we** all, with open face beholding as in a glass the glory of the Lord, **are changed into the same image** from glory to glory, even as by the Spirit of the Lord.*

_____

OUR ATTITUDE—"BUT WE ALL, WITH OPEN FACE"

    a. "We all"—This change is available to every Christian who is willing to meet the criteria.

    b. "with open face"—Picture a young person with an open face and another with a brash, hard face. The concept of "open face" seems to denote a continued openness to God's leadership and an eager expectation of His help.

"It is only as we are ready . . . to fully live in the obedience to the voice of God and the faith of Jesus, that our life can grow."—Andrew Murray in *Holiest of All*

Remember, the Lord is patient with our ignorance. An open relationship with Him demands surrender to all He has shown us to this point in our walk with Him.

OUR ACTION—"BEHOLDING AS IN A GLASS THE GLORY OF THE LORD"

The word *glory* means "brilliant light." No human can look at God's glory and live because His glory is so bright. God has diffused His glory to us in this world through the prism of time. We will never see the full glory of God's face until we get to heaven, but we can see Him through "mirrors" in this life:

    a. In the Bible   c. In Spirit-filled preaching

    b. In other Spirit-filled Christians   d. In God's sovereign hand through the circumstances of life

A man doesn't gaze into his wife's face just to memorize her features but to enjoy her beauty. Neither do we read our Bibles just to obtain facts regarding God but to behold and appreciate the beauty of His holiness. Will you begin to focus your attention on the glory of God?

OUR ALTERATION—"ARE CHANGED INTO THE SAME IMAGE FROM GLORY TO GLORY"

Notice it does not say that we change ourselves but that we are changed. This is a continual process of being changed. The Greek word translated *changed* is the origin of our word *metamorphosis*. God's desire is to change us progressively and thoroughly from the inside out. This is the same Greek word that is translated *transformed* in Romans 12:2.

OUR AGENT—"EVEN AS BY THE SPIRIT OF THE LORD"

As long as we look to the Lord in surrendered dependence, God's Holy Spirit, Who lives in us, continues to do His changing work to our life. **One of my greatest confidences in this life is the Christian's ability to change.**

11. How does God promise to give us the ability to say no to our lusts?

    Galatians 5:16—This I say then, **Walk in the Spirit,** *and [you] shall not fulfil the lust of the flesh.*

The implication of the context of this passage is that these two things are mutually exclusive. It is not possible to fulfill the lust of the flesh if you are walking in the Spirit.

One might ask, "How do I walk in the Spirit?" Walking is nothing more than a series of reiterated steps. Walking in the Spirit is simply taking one spiritual step after another. Trusting Christ to save you from sin and hell was a step of faith. You knew you could not save yourself. You knew He died in your place and would save you if you chose to depend on Him alone for salvation. Now you can walk in the Spirit the same way. Every time you need to make a decision or need strength to do right, simply look to Him in dependence and He will give you the grace you need for the occasion. "As you have therefore received Christ Jesus the Lord, so walk . . . in him" (Colossians 2:6).

This process may not be exactly what you think it is. Many people think His strength in us makes us inherently strong when we depend on Him. The reality is that our flesh stays with us until the day we go to live with Jesus forever in heaven. What He promises to give us is not inherent power but overcoming power. Remember when we likened the law of sin to the law of gravity—neither will go away. Remember too that we likened the promised victory in Christ to the counteracting potential of aerodynamics. As long as I am safe in a functional airplane, I can rise to amazing heights without any danger from the effects of gravity. God does not remove the law of sin from our flesh. He simply gives us power to overcome its effects by keeping our trust focused on Him.

12. Numbers 21:6–9 gives us an illustration of God's overcoming power and how it works. The Bible teaches us that God's people were plagued by snakes that were killing the people.

> *Numbers 21:7–9—Therefore the people came to Moses, and said . . . pray unto the Lord, that **he take away the serpents from us**. And Moses prayed for the people. And the Lord said unto Moses, Make . . . a fiery serpent, and set it upon a pole: and it shall come to pass, that every one that is bitten, when he [looks] upon it, shall live. And Moses made a serpent of brass, and put it upon a pole, and it came to pass, that if a serpent had bitten any man, when he beheld the serpent of brass, he lived.*

What did the people want God to do?

_____

Did God provide for the safety of the people?

_____

Was it what the people asked for?

_____

He didn't get rid of the snakes. He gave the people an antidote for the snakes' power over them. When the people chose to depend on the truth of God's promise to keep them from the power of a serpent bite and looked at the brass serpent in faith, a tangible, but invisible power was given to them for health. This same tangible, invisible power is what He promises you. In John 3:14 Jesus likens Himself to this serpent in the wilderness. It doesn't "make sense" to our material mindset, but **God dispenses victory through giving strength to anyone who simply will choose to act on His promises and look to His grace for the victory.**

The Christian life is compared to running a marathon. God asks three things of us in order to help us run with endurance. What are they?

> *Hebrews 12:1–2—Wherefore seeing we also are compassed about with so great a cloud of witnesses, [a]**let us lay aside every weight, and** the **sin** which [does] so easily beset us, and [b]**let us run with patience** the race that is set before us, [c]**looking unto Jesus the author and finisher of our faith**; who for the joy that was set before him endured the cross, despising the shame, and is set down at the right hand of the throne of God.*

a.

_____

b.

_____

c.

_____

Who initiates and completes our faith?

_____

Weight—things that are not necessarily wrong but hinder our progress

Patience—persistent endurance

Looking—fixing our eyes steadfastly upon

Write your understanding of one of the following illustrations and how it applies to your life. (Feel free to look back at your notes.)

The Law of Aerodynamics Overcoming the Pull of Gravity – page 34

Corrective Lenses Overcoming the Condition of Myopia – page 39

Fire Overcoming the Characteristics of Cold Iron – page 41

A Bright Light Overcoming the Tendency of a Dark Room – page 41

The Story of Mr. Fact, Mr. Faith, and Mr. Feeling – page 54

_____

_____

_____

_____

_____

_____

_____

_____

In each illustration, what happens when a person stops depending on God's overcoming power?

_____

We experience the Spirit-filled life as we choose to invite Jesus to rule as Lord in our life and depend on His power to live victoriously. It grows and is maintained as we continue in surrendered dependence. The Christian walk is not one of struggling to succeed through the energies of the flesh, but resting in His offered grace.

> *Matthew 11:28–30—Come unto me, all [you] that labour and are heavy laden, and **I will give you rest**. Take my yoke upon you, and learn of me; for I am meek and lowly in heart: and [you] shall find rest unto your souls. For **my yoke is easy, and my burden is light**.*

APPLICATION

James 1:22–25 promises God's special blessing on those who take action on what His Word teaches.

In this lesson you have seen that sin is damaging to the Christian life, and we have no ability to overcome its overwhelming control by our own self-efforts. God's overcoming power is your only hope. You must stay focused on Him. It is a matter of depending on the promises of God while not allowing yourself to be deceived by "**the deceitfulness of sin.**" If you have a sin that is between you and the Lord, will you confess it right now? Are there any "weights" that the Lord has burdened your heart about? Again, it is not a matter of pleading for victory but of resting on the victory God has already provided. There is no other. Will you continue to depend on Him for victory today and forever?

In the space below write your resolve in the form of a prayer.

_____

_____

_____

_____

_____

_____

_____

_____

Caution: It is possible to become too introspective and to look for a sin problem every time you *feel* guilty or *sense* that something is wrong with your relationship with God. The Bible teaches that Satan is a deceiver and the accuser of the brethren, and he has the ability to deceive Christians in this area. One way to tell the difference between the confusion of the Devil and the conviction of the Holy Spirit is to identify the type of conviction you are experiencing. The Holy Spirit deals with us in a specific manner so that we know exactly what the problem is and exactly what we need to do. Confession of that kind of sin gives immediate relief and restoration of His love, joy, peace, and so forth. The Devil's false conviction is often a general feeling of guilt and uneasiness. Some experience guilt concerning something in the past that has already been confessed. Confession of that kind of sin gives no relief and never can. (How to defeat the Devil will be further discussed in lesson 8.)

ASSIGNMENTS

Bible Reading: Matthew 22–28

Scripture Memory:

> *Galatians 5:16—This I say then, Walk in the Spirit, and [you] shall not fulfil the lust of the flesh.*

> [This verse is part of *The Exchange* Scripture Memory System.]

Practical Assignment: Read Ephesians 4–5:17 and record the five ways a Spirit-filled Christian walks differently from a Christian who is not Spirit-filled.

1. _____

2. _____

3. _____

4. _____

5. _____

Ephesians 5:18 states, "And be not drunk with wine, wherein is excess; but be filled with the Spirit." Read Ephesians 5:19–6:12 and record at least three areas of life changed by being filled with the Holy Spirit.

_____

_____

_____

LESSON 8

THE HOLY SPIRIT AND MY CHANGING LIFE

HOW TO LIVE AS A SPIRIT-FILLED CHRISTIAN IN A SINFUL WORLD

By now you have discovered that life is different from what it was before you became a Christian. This lesson is about the changes you can expect and how to understand and adjust to those changes.

UNDERSTANDING THE INTERNAL CHANGE

1. How does God expect believers to walk?

   *Ephesians 2:8–10—For by grace are [you] saved through faith; and that not of yourselves: it is the gift of God: not of works, lest any man should boast. For **we are his workmanship, created in Christ Jesus unto good works**, which **God** [has] before **ordained that we should walk in them**.*

   _____

2. Find the five ways Spirit-filled Christians should walk, and circle them.

   Ephesians 4:1—I . . . beseech you that [you] walk worthy of the vocation wherewith [you] are called.

   Ephesians 4:17—This I say therefore, and testify in the Lord, that you henceforth walk not as other Gentiles walk, in the vanity of their mind.

   Ephesians 5:2—And walk in love, as Christ also [has] loved us, and [has] given himself for us an offering and a sacrifice to God for a sweet-smelling savour [fragrance].

   Ephesians 5:8—For [you] were sometimes darkness, but now are [you] light in the Lord: walk as children of light.

   Ephesians 5:15—See then that [you] walk circumspectly [watching each step carefully so as not to defile yourself], not as fools, but as wise.

Taking off and putting on a garment is another picture of the Spirit-filled life and your ability to walk differently from your unsaved counterparts.

3. Describe the garment God commands you to take off.

*Ephesians 4:22—That [you] put off concerning the former conversation [lifestyle] **the old man**, which is **corrupt** according to the **deceitful lusts** [desires].*

_____

4. What happened to our old man?

*Romans 6:6—Knowing this, that **our old man is crucified with him**, that the body of sin might be destroyed, that henceforth we should not serve sin.*

_____

Your unregenerate spirit, which could never please God, is dead. However, the residual influence of that old nature still remains in your lifestyle. You have formed patterns of behavior that your flesh is loathe to give up. When you got saved, God rewired you, so to speak. As a result of the exchange you made with Jesus, you are connected to God's vast spiritual resources, and His enabling grace flows through you as you surrender. When you say no to God, it not only disconnects you from God's overcoming power but causes you to resort to your own strength and desires. Picture two drinking cups. If you choose to go your own way, you effectively take your "straw" out of the Spirit's cup and begin drawing from the cup of your flesh. As long as you have your "straw" in the Spirit, you will draw on His power and produce His fruit. The power of the flesh is strong, but it does not control you as your unregenerate spirit did. You have been freed from its control. Taking off the old man is to consider it crucified with Jesus, and choosing not to follow its residual influence on your flesh.

What does God call your choice to draw from the resources of your flesh instead of your regenerated spirit?

Jeremiah 2:13—For my people have committed two evils; they have forsaken me the fountain of living waters, and hewed them out cisterns, broken cisterns, that can hold no water.

_____

5. Describe the garment God wants you to put on.

*Ephesians 4:24—And that [you] put on **the new man**, which after God is **created in righteousness** and **true holiness**.*

_____

Before receiving Christ, your "old man" [unregenerate spirit] had complete sway over your soul. You were alive to sin but dead to Christ. Your 'new man' [regenerated spirit] was born in you at the moment of salvation. Until then, there was only one "man" your soul could wear. Your old man could not do anything that pleased God. Even the "plowing of the wicked is sin" (Proverbs 21:4). Your new man is your connection to spiritual living. Notice what is said concerning your new man. You are made after God, that is, in His image. Only God is righteous and truly holy. These characteristics are divine in nature. Therefore, your new man is God-like and is perfectly right with God. It is God's seed in you that cannot sin (1 John 3:9). The new man is not the Holy Spirit but is **born** of the Spirit and **empowered** by the Spirit. What satisfies God satisfies your new man. Never forget—**this new man is the new you**, recreated in God's image. The reason you loathe the sin you still commit from time to time is that it conflicts with your new nature.

Every new Christian has had this experience. Perhaps you recall doing something that was part of your old life. You may remember that horrible feeling of wondering, "What is wrong with me?" and feeling like a horrible failure. That was a wonderful moment! Your new nature was making its debut in its life-long pursuit of transforming your life into the image of Christ.

6. What must you be convinced is true about you?

    Romans 6:11—Likewise reckon . . . also yourselves to be dead indeed unto sin, but alive unto God through Jesus Christ our Lord.

    _____

As death to the old man is a disconnection from its controlling power, so being alive to God is connecting to His power, which enables you to obey. When you trusted Christ to save you, He realigned your relationship with spiritual life and death. You were once connected to sin and death with no ability to break free. Now you are connected to God and His holy life.

7. If one nature is "old" and one is "new," and if one is "dead" and the other is "born again," which nature characterizes who you are now that you are in Christ?

    _____

8. Did God give you new desires when He realigned your life?

    2 Corinthians 5:17—Therefore if any man be in Christ, he is a new creature: old things are passed away; behold, all things are become new.

    _____

9. Describe the residual patterns and desires your crucified "old man" left in your flesh.

    Ephesians 4:22—That [you] put off concerning the former conversation the old man, which is corrupt according to the deceitful lusts [desires].

    _____

The flesh is still able to deceive you into giving place to old desires. The word translated *lust* from the original language is closely related to the modern word *thermos*. The picture is of insulating and inflaming an ungodly thought or desire until it catches fire and burns us.

10. What happens when an ungodly thought or desire is inflamed?

    James 1:15—Then when lust [has] conceived, it [brings] forth sin: and sin, when it is finished, [brings] forth death.

    _____

What follows?

    _____

One could call this the **LSD** principle. **L**ust, when it is insulated and inflamed, produces **S**in. This is not something that **might** happen when you give in to lust but something that **will** happen every time. Sin always brings **D**eath back into your life. This death is not cessation of spiritual life but separation from its power. When you sin, you have ceased to allow the Holy Spirit to control every thought and action and cannot be filled with the Spirit until you deal with your sin. You must put off the influence of the old man before the energizing power of the new man can be renewed (Ephesians 4:22–24). This cannot be done through human effort alone but must be the work of Jesus, accessed by genuine confession of sin (1 John 1:9) and demonstrated by forsaking that sin. The rest of Ephesians 4 gives practical application of the change this brings to a life. It is important to note that sin does not change our legal standing with God. In fact, God likens our relationship with Him to the relationship of an earthly father and his sometimes-disobedient child. The sin of a Christian does not place him back under eternal condemnation, but it does take him out of intimate fellowship with God.

11. What should a disobedient Christian expect?

    Hebrews 12:6–7—For whom the Lord [loves] **he [chastens]**, *and [scourges]* **every son** *whom he [receives]. . . .* **God [deals] with you as with sons;** *for what son is he whom the father [chastens] not?*

    _____

12. Why does He chastise us?

    Hebrews 12:10—For they [earthly fathers] verily for a few days chastened us after their own pleasure; but he [chastens us] **for our profit, that we might be partakers of his holiness.**

    _____

Though you are still His child, sin changes your fellowship with Him. When you choose to disobey, you are taking back control of your own life. You have decided that you know better than God.

13. Do you remember what happens to those who are proud?

    James 4:6— **God [resists] the proud,** *but [gives] grace unto the humble.*

    _____

When you have said no to God, you take your life off the altar of sacrifice. You have invited God's siege of resistance and are disconnected from the unrestricted supply of His Spirit's power. You will be stuck in a pattern of spiritual battle against God with no ability to do anything that pleases Him until you rid yourself of rebellion and look to Him to reestablish the flow of His grace in your life.

This destructive pattern comes from **deceitful** lusts. The realigning that Christ did in us at the point of salvation gave us a new nature that takes no pleasure in sin. It certainly doesn't satisfy. Then why do we go back to sin? The problem is that we are deceived.

14. Since the problem is **deceit**, the answer lies in the **truth**. What did Jesus say about the truth?

    John 8:32—And [you] shall know the truth, and **the truth shall make you free.**

    _____

Though our unregenerate spirit is gone, its lifestyle still resides in our flesh and God has commanded us to put it off. He has also commanded us to draw on the resources of our regenerated spirit, which was recreated in the image of God.

The fact that we are required to choose between the two indicates that another part exists that has the ability to choose. That other part is our Soul, often described as our mind, emotions, and will. These are stated in this order due to logical sequence. First, you think about what you should or should not do; then you set your affections one way or the other; and finally you most often choose that way for which your affections have been cast.

It should be noted that emotions are not easily controlled and are often misleading. Remember the Mr. Fact, Mr. Feelings, and Mr. Faith illustration. We rarely "feel" our way into a right action, and feelings often take awhile to come around to right decisions. The key is our will. We must choose to draw from the resources of our regenerated spirit.

15. What does God tell us to do with our mind?

    *Ephesians 4:23—And **be renewed in the spirit of your mind**.*

    _____

16. What kind of mind do you have now that you are saved?

    *2 Timothy 1:7—For **God has** not **given us the spirit** of fear; but of power, and of love, and **of a sound mind**.*

    _____

To have the victory the Lord provides, you must personally reckon these statements to be true and choose to depend on them. This is the way you use the truth of God's Word to give you freedom from the deceitful influence of the old man.

17. How can you engraft God's Word into the way you think?

    *James 1:21—Wherefore lay apart all filthiness and superfluity [abundance] of naughtiness, and receive with meekness the engrafted word, **which is able to save your souls**.*

    _____

    What motivates you to engraft God's Word into your mind?

    _____

Trying to draw on the resources of the flesh and our regenerated spirit at the same time will only flood our soul with conflicting messages and will ultimately lead to defeat. The clear message of God's Word is able to save us from this double-mindedness. There are times for all of us when the troubles of life and heartaches of soul wear us down. During those times you will be vulnerable to sin's attack. There may be times you don't seem to be able to think right about sin and victory. The problem may be that you have a sick soul. No one feels good when he's sick. When you go to a doctor who discovers the problem and prescribes the right medicine, feeling good never felt so good. The right medicine for a sick soul is the Word of God. Allowing the Holy Spirit to use the Bible to center your mind on Christ is the need of your heart.

Hebrews 12:3—For consider him that endured such contradiction of sinners against himself, lest you be wearied [sick] and faint [let go] in your minds [souls].

18. What kind of weaponry has God provided for the Christian?

    *2 Corinthians 10:3–4 For though we walk in the flesh, we do not war after [in the ability of] the flesh: (**for the weapons of our warfare are** not carnal [fleshly], but **mighty** [supernatural] **through God** to the pulling down of strong holds).*

    _____

19. What will the Holy Spirit enable us to do?

    *2 Corinthians 10:5—Casting down imaginations, and every high thing that [exalts] itself against the knowledge of God, and **bringing into captivity every thought to the obedience of Christ**.*

    _____

20. Once your thinking is right, what will God enable you to do with your affections?

    *Colossians 3:2—**Set your affection on things above**, not on things on the earth.*

    _____

21. Who can you count on to give you the willpower to do right?

    *Philippians 2:13—For it is God which [works] in you **both to will and to do of his good pleasure**.*

    _____

UNDERSTANDING THE EXTERNAL AND INTERNAL ENEMIES

If deception is the problem, who or what is doing the deceiving? The Bible teaches that we have three enemies constantly pulling at us to do wrong: our flesh, the world and the Devil. We dealt with the first two in other lessons. Now we will meet the third enemy, the power behind the other two.

22. Your primary enemy is an invisible spirit, nevertheless, a real person. What is his name?

    *1 Peter 5:8—Be sober, be vigilant; because **your adversary the devil**, as a roaring lion, [walks] about, seeking whom he may devour.*

    _____

23. What two terms describe his character and indicate his methods?

    *John 8:44—The devil . . . was **a murderer** from the beginning, and abode not in the truth, because there is no truth in him. When he [speaks] a lie, he [speaks] of his own: for he is **a liar**, and the father of it.*

    _____

UNDERSTANDING THE PERSON OF VICTORY

24. What is the key to running the marathon God set before you?

   *Hebrews 12:1–2—Let us lay aside every weight, and the sin which [does] so easily beset us, and let us run with patience the race that is set before us, **looking unto Jesus** the author and finisher of our faith; who for the joy that was set before him endured the cross, despising the shame, and is set down at the right hand of the throne of God.*

   _____

Though it takes diligence and perseverance, the victorious Christ-life is very simple: just keep your eyes focused on Jesus. He is the answer to transformed living.

25. What was Paul afraid the Corinthian Christians would lose through Satan's deception?

   *2 Corinthians 11:3—But I fear, lest by any means, as the serpent beguiled Eve through his subtilty, so **your minds should be corrupted from the simplicity that is in Christ.***

   _____

26. What does God promise to those who are tempted?

   *1 Corinthians 10:13—There [has] no temptation taken you but such as is common to man: but God is faithful, who will not suffer you to be tempted above that [you] are able; but will with the temptation also make **a way to escape, that [you] may be able to bear it**.*

   _____

27. How can you avoid temptations?

   *Romans 13:14—But **put . . . on the Lord Jesus Christ**, and **make not provision for the flesh**, to fulfil the lusts thereof.*

   _____

UNDERSTANDING THE LIFE OF VICTORY

28. What two attributes characterize the "new man"?

   *Ephesians 4:24—And that [you] put on the new man, which after God is created in **righteousness** and true **holiness**.*

   _____

Righteousness is perfectly fulfilling God's law; holiness is separateness from sin. Though only God is holy, He has placed His holiness in our regenerated spirit when we were born again. When we live out of the resources of our new man, we are living out of the resources of His nature: "Christ in you the hope of glory" (Colossians 1:27).

To what extent does God intend your new life to be holy?

   *1 Peter 1:15—But as he which [has] called you is holy, so be [you] holy **in all manner of conversation [lifestyle]**.*

29. What promise is given to those who decide to obey God by separating from evil?

*2 Corinthians 6:14–17—Be not unequally yoked together with unbelievers: for what fellowship [has] righteousness with unrighteousness? and what communion [has] light with darkness? And what concord [has] Christ with Belial [the Devil]? or what part [has] he that [believes] with an infidel? And what agreement [has] the temple of God with idols? for you are the temple of the living God; as God [has] said, **I will dwell in them, and walk in them**; and **I will be their God**, and **they shall be my people**. Wherefore come out from among them, and be . . . separate, [says] the Lord, and touch not the unclean thing; and **I will receive you**.*

_____

Consider how important it is for a doctor to wear gloves to prevent contamination. He can ignore the obvious dangers, or he can stay away from danger by not caring for people at all. He chooses, however, to both care for the needs of his patients and avoid contamination by wearing protective gloves. The world we live in is a sinful place that is hostile to Spirit-filled living, yet it is filled with many needy people. Obviously, during this lifetime, God's plan is not to completely withdraw from the world. His will for us is to live in this world, helping sinful men, all the while protecting ourselves by separating from sin through the promised overcoming power of the Holy Spirit.

APPLICATION

30. Check the area(s) in which you now fail to bring glory to God because you are pressured by the world, drawn down by your own desires, or tempted by Satan:

☐ **Attitudes**   ☐ **Drugs/substance abuse**   ☐ **Entertainment**

☐ **Sexual Conduct**   ☐ **Language**   ☐ **Music**

☐ **Appearance**   ☐ **Other** _____

31. Should you wait for some "special conviction" from God before you obey what His Word says about your attitudes, appearance, and actions?

*James 1:22—But **be doers** of the word, and not hearers only, deceiving your own selves.*

*James 4:7—**Submit yourselves** therefore to God. Resist the devil, and he will flee from you.*

_____

James 1:22–25 promises God's special blessing on those who take action on what His Word teaches.

In this lesson you have seen that you have lifestyle patterns from your old man to put off and a new man to put on. The sinful person you used to be no longer characterizes you. You are now identified as a new man. God's grace enables you to live your new life in the righteousness and true holiness of your new man. **Spirituality is not measured primarily by what you do and don't do. Spiritual living is surrendered dependence upon the Holy Spirit.** When Jesus lives His life through you, His righteousness will be manifested in your life.

You are growing in your awareness of Who the Lord is and how you can count on Him to change your life. Has the Lord shown you any area in which you need to expect Him to give you victory? In the space provided, write your resolve in the form of a prayer.

_____

_____

_____

_____

_____

_____

ASSIGNMENTS

Bible Reading: Acts 1–7

Scripture Memory:

> *2 Corinthians 5:17—Therefore if any man be in Christ, he is a new creature: old things are passed away; behold, all things are become new.*

(This verse is part of *The Exchange* Scripture Memory System.)

Practical Assignment: Have there been noticeable changes in your life since you accepted Christ? This is the work of the Lord, and He should receive the glory for it. Write a specific prayer of praise for each area of change He has made in your life.

_____

_____

_____

_____

_____

_____

_____

As you have done this Bible study, the Lord has begun to show you areas of your life He desires to change. Write them down and ask the Lord to show you truths from His Word concerning each area.

_____

_____

_____

_____

_____

_____

_____

_____

_____

_____

_____

_____

_____

LESSON 9

THE HOLY SPIRIT AND MY PRAYER LIFE

HOW TO ACCESS GOD'S THRONE OF GRACE

Prayer is one of God's greatest inheritance gifts. Jesus taught that we can move mountains through prayer. Through the ages, men of God have accomplished through prayer what never could have been done without it. God desires that every one of His children come to Him in prayer. Prayer is asking of God and receiving from Him. It leads to God-dependence rather than self-dependence. Prayer can stop our natural bent to trust in our own thinking and abilities to meet our needs and leads us to let God direct our lives and provide for us. In this lesson we will look at the definition and description of prayer, confirm the importance of prayer, deal with hindrances to prayer, and learn how to pray.

WHAT IS PRAYER?

The Christian life is not religious acts or personal performances. It is a dynamic, intimate relationship with God. Communication is the most vital need of a growing relationship. God speaks to us as we read and study our Bibles, listen to preaching, and so forth. Prayer is talking to God and is essential for living in a close relationship with Him.

Prayer is not just a ceremony we memorize and perform. It is a lifeline in the communication chain we share with God. Our primary relationship with God is a receiving relationship. Prayer is not a duty; it is a gift. Prayer is the means by which God implements His provision.

1. What does God invite us to do?

   *1 Peter 5:7—**Casting all your care upon him**; for he [cares] for you.*

   _____

   Why?

   _____

God already knows all that is in your heart, but He invites you to open your heart to Him and give Him your burdens. He loves drawing you close in this way, making your relationship with Him dynamic and intimate. What an awesome gift that we unworthy souls are invited to be close to Deity!

Prayer also includes listening to God. In this lesson you will learn the importance of praying in the will of God. One of the most wonderful aspects of our communion with the Holy Spirit is that He communicates to us, thereby allowing us to align ourselves with His will and actually participate in bringing it about.

2. Jesus taught His disciples about prayer by teaching them the Lord's Prayer.

   Matthew 6:9–10—Our Father which art in heaven, hallowed be thy name. Thy kingdom come. Thy will be done in earth, as it is in heaven.

   Where does God's will originate?

   _____

   How do we get God's will down to earth?

   _____

3. Who are we in our relationship with Jesus?

   *Romans 8:16–17—The Spirit itself [bears] witness with our spirit, that we are the children of God: and if children, then heirs; **heirs of God**, and **joint-heirs with Christ**.*

   _____

During Jesus' earthly ministry, He spent many hours talking to His Father and receiving comfort and guidance from Him. As God's heirs, one of our inheritance rights is the privilege to talk to Him and have Him meet our needs through prayer.

4. What does this verse tell us about the ministry of prayer for today?

   *John 16:26–27—At that day [you] shall ask in my name: and I say not unto you, that I will pray the Father for you: for the **Father himself [loves] you**, because [you] have loved me, and have believed that I came out from God.*

   _____

In His teaching ministry Jesus painted a picture of prayer by describing a loving father's provision for his impatient, hungry child. He began with a wonderful invitation and promise.

   Luke 11:9—And I say unto you, Ask, and it shall be given you; seek, and [you] shall find; knock, and it shall be opened unto you.

Notice that He emphasized the teaching by saying that everyone who asks, receives; everyone who seeks, finds, and everyone who knocks, it will be opened to him.

   Luke 11:10—For every one that [asks receives]; and he that [seeks finds]; and to him that [knocks] it shall be opened.

The listeners in Jesus' day who had traveled many miles on foot in the surrounding wilderness better understood the following statements:

Luke 11:11–13—If a son shall ask bread of any of you that is a father, will he give him a stone? or if he ask a fish, will he for a fish give him a serpent? Or if he shall ask an egg, will he offer him a scorpion? If [you] then, being evil, know how to give good gifts unto your children, how much more shall your heavenly Father give the Holy Spirit to them that ask him?

Jesus asked the fathers which of them would give a stone to his hungry son who was asking for bread. The connection between the two seemingly unconnected items would be immediate for those who had seen beside the road the stones that looked exactly like a loaf of bread, the serpent moving in the water as a fish, or the scorpion rolled up to look like an egg. No father would give his impatient, hungry little one the stone that the child, in his immaturity, thought was a loaf of bread. The father would remind his child that he must wait until something appropriate to eat was available. He loved his son; so, of course, he would feed him.

Luke 11:13—How much more shall your heavenly Father give the Holy Spirit to them that ask him?

Jesus made it very clear that God is your heavenly Father and that He most certainly will give you the power of the Holy Spirit for specific needs when you ask for it. **God does answer your prayers.** However, He loves you enough not to give you "the rock" you asked for but will surely give you "the bread" you need.

5. What are the two words repeated in each of these verses?

   *Matthew 7:8—For every one that **[asks receives]**; and he that [seeks finds]; and to him that [knocks] it shall be opened.*

   *Matthew 21:22—And all things, whatsoever [you] shall **ask** in prayer, believing, [you] shall **receive**.*

   *Luke 11:10—For every one that **[asks receives]**; and he that [seeks finds]; and to him that [knocks] it shall be opened.*

   *John 16:24—Hitherto have [you] **asked** nothing in my name: **ask**, and [you] shall **receive**, that your joy may be full.*

   *James 4:3—[You] **ask**, and **receive** not, because [you] **ask** amiss, that [you] may consume it upon your lusts.*

   *1 John 3:22—And whatsoever we **ask**, we **receive** of him, because we keep his commandments, and do those things that are pleasing in his sight.*

   _____

   Do you get the idea that when we ask for something from God we should expect to receive it?

   _____

A great book on prayer entitled *Asking and Receiving* reminds us that prayer is more than just asking God for things. Biblical prayer is asking **and receiving**.

6. What spiritual place do we enter when we pray?

   *Hebrews 4:16—Let us therefore come boldly **unto the throne of grace**, that we may obtain mercy, and find grace to help in time of need.*

   _____

Prayer is communication with God that accomplishes God's heavenly plans for our lives here on earth. It is drawing close to Him and trusting Him as a loving Father. Prayer is not complete when we are finished asking; it is complete when we see God answer our prayer. We are children of the King, and He has invited us into His very throne room to seek His amazing grace and marvelous mercy every time we need Him. And we need Him all the time.

THE IMPORTANCE OF PRAYER

7. Ephesians 6:12–19 deals with our spiritual warfare. Notice the "all's" in this verse. In your own words record the importance prayer plays in securing victory over the enemy.

    *Ephesians 6:18—Praying **always** with **all prayer** and **supplication** in the Spirit, and watching thereunto with **all perseverance** and supplication for **all** saints.*

    _____

    _____

8. Prayer is God's appointed way of obtaining what we need. What happens when we don't pray?

    *James 4:2—[You] . . . desire to have, and cannot obtain . . . yet [you] **have not, because** [you] **ask not**.*

    _____

9. When the early church had a problem, too many responsibilities and too few workers, how did the apostles view the importance of prayer?

    *Acts 6:4—But **we will give ourselves continually to prayer**, and to the ministry of the word.*

    _____

10. The word *prayer* is used over twenty-five times in conjunction with Jesus' earthly ministry. Record the time of day Jesus was seen praying.

    *Mark 1:35—And **in the morning**, rising up **a great while before day**, he went out, and departed into a solitary place, and there prayed.*

    _____

    *Luke 6:12—And it came to pass in those days, that he went out into a mountain to pray, and **continued all night in prayer** to God.*

    _____

Prayer is also important in our lives because it promotes spiritual growth!

11. In the beginning of this psalm, David praised the Lord for knowing Him thoroughly. What did he ask God to do to help his walk with God?

    *Psalm 139:23–24—**Search me**, O God, and know my heart: **try me**, and know my thoughts: and **see if there be any wicked way in me**, and **lead me in the way everlasting**.*

    _____

12. What else is available through prayer?

    *Psalm 51:7—**Purge me** with hyssop, and **I shall be clean: wash me**, and **I shall be whiter than snow**.*

    _____

13. What is God willing to do in response to prayer?

    *Psalm 119:18—**Open . . . mine eyes**, that I may behold wondrous things out of [Your] law.*

    _____

    *James 1:5—If any of you lack **wisdom**, let him ask of God, that [gives] to all men liberally, and [upbraids] not; and it **shall be given** him.*

    _____

14. Please note the areas of growth mentioned in these verses.

    *John 16:24—Hitherto have [you] asked nothing in my name: ask, and [you] shall receive, that your **joy** may be full.*

    _____

    *Philippians 4:6—Be careful [**anxious**] for nothing; but in every thing by prayer and supplication with thanksgiving let your requests be made known unto God.*

    _____

    *Luke 11:13—If [you] then, being evil, know how to give good gifts unto your children: how much more shall your heavenly Father give the **Holy Spirit** [power] to them that ask him?*

    _____

    *Luke 21:34, 36—And take heed to yourselves, lest at any time your hearts be overcharged with surfeiting [predrunkenness], and drunkenness, and cares of this life. . . . Watch . . . therefore, and pray always, that [you] may be accounted worthy to **escape all these things** that shall come to pass, and to stand before the Son of man.*

    _____

HOW TO PRAY

15. Though many enjoy praying the Lord's Prayer as a memorized prayer, it was actually given as a model by which to construct our own personal prayers to God. Notice the different parts of the prayer and in your own words title each section.

    Matthew 6:9–13—After this manner therefore pray ye: Our Father which art in heaven.

    _____

    Hallowed be thy name.

    _____

    Thy kingdom come. Thy will be done in earth, as it is in heaven.

    _____

Give us this day our daily bread.

_____

And forgive us our debts,

_____

As we forgive our debtors.

_____

And lead us not into temptation, but deliver us from evil:

_____

For thine is the kingdom, and the power, and the glory, for ever. Amen.

_____

Following are titles I have given each section. Use this as a model to write your own sample prayer.

Address God and recognize His Sovereignty.

_____

Praise Him as God.

_____

Pray to know and do the will of God.

_____

Pray for personal and practical needs.

_____

Confess any unconfessed sins. (If you can't think of any, ask God to reveal any sins that He wants you to confess.)

_____

Pray a prayer of forgiveness concerning anyone who has wronged you. (If the situation is known to the person you are praying for, you may need to forgive him directly.)

_____

Pray for spiritual power and for victory over sin.

_____

Praise and adore God. (Jesus begins and ends this model prayer with praise. Praise is a great way to prepare your heart in prayer, but you will find that your praise is more vibrant and your worship more personal as you end your prayer with praise.)

In the late eighteenth century George Müller, a great man of prayer, started and ran several orphanages. The following is an excerpt from a biography by J. Gilchrist Lawson (www.wholesomewords.org).

> Among the greatest monuments of what can be accomplished through simple faith in God are the great orphanages covering thirteen acres of ground on Ashley Down, Bristol, England. When God put it into the heart of George Müller to build these orphanages, he had only two shillings (50 cents) in his pocket. Without making his wants known to any man, but to God alone, over a million, four hundred thousand pounds ($7,000,000.00) were sent to him for the building and maintaining of these orphan homes. When [Lawson] first visited them, near the time of Mr. Müller's death, there were five immense buildings of solid granite, capable of accommodating two thousand orphans. In all the years since the first orphans arrived, the Lord had sent food in due time so that they had never missed a meal for want of food.

Müller purposed to give the church a working picture of the power of God demonstrated by simply praying. When funds were low, he would often spend the night in prayer, looking for a specific promise in the Word of God to claim and expect God to keep.

16. Psalm 81:10 was one of Müller's favorite verses. Can you think of anything you should pray for based on this promise?

    Psalm 81:10—I am the Lord [your] God, which brought [you] out of the land of Egypt: open [your] mouth wide, and I will fill it.

    _____

    _____

    _____

17. Can you think of any other promises from the Word of God you can take to the Lord? Record them in the space below. If you can't think of any, ask God to show you some as you read your Bible over the next several days.

    Hosea 14:2—Take with you words, and turn to the Lord.

    _____

    _____

    _____

I like to call this "praying the promises." Promises from God are invitations to pray. Through these promises God is telling us what He wants to do, and is, in effect, inviting us to be the prayer channels by which He can accomplish His will here on earth.

18. How can we have confidence that God is hearing us and will answer our prayer?

*1 John 5:14–15—And this is the confidence that we have in Him, that, if we **ask** any thing **according to his will**, he [hears] us: and if we know that he hear us, whatsoever we ask, we know that we have the petitions that we desired of him.*

The next logical question is how we can know what God's will is. The Bible is the complete, authoritative revelation of God's person and truth to man. It is all we need to know about Who God is, who we are, and how to have a right relationship with Him—including what He wants to do in our lives. R. A. Torrey once said, "If we would feed the fire of our prayers with the fuel of God's Word, all of our difficulties in prayer would disappear."

The Bible teaches God's will in all the general areas of life; but there are other specific areas, unique to your life, that He also wants to show you.

19. Who lives in you now that you are a Christian?

*Romans 8:11—But if the **Spirit of him** that raised up Jesus from the dead **dwell in you**, he that raised up Christ from the dead shall also quicken [give life to] your mortal bodies by his Spirit that [dwells] in you.*

---

20. How does the Holy Spirit communicate to us that we are adopted into God's family and that we should cry out to Him as our intimate Father?

*Romans 8:14–16—For as many as are led by the Spirit of God, they are the sons of God. For [you] have not received the spirit of bondage again to fear; but [you] have received **the Spirit** of adoption, **whereby we cry, Abba, Father**. **The Spirit** itself **[bears] witness with our spirit**, that we are the children of God.*

This terminology indicates that the Holy Spirit is issuing a joint statement with your regenerated spirit that you are the child of God, and when your soul is in tune with Him, it is stirred to intimately cry out to your heavenly Father. When my wife and I were in Israel, we visited the headwaters of the Jordan River. It was a holiday, and the natural pool of water was filled with Israeli children splashing and playing in the heat of the day. The hum of a foreign language filled our ears, but one word of recognition clearly rang out as the children cried over and over, "Abba, Abba." It brought tears to our eyes as we recognized the familiar intimacy of that word to those happy children. The blessed Holy Spirit creates a longing for intimacy with our heavenly Father and stirs our hearts to cry out to Him.

21. Does God know that we don't always know what we should pray?

*Romans 8:26–27—Likewise the Spirit also [helps] our infirmities [weaknesses]: for **we know not what we should pray** for as we ought: but the Spirit itself [makes] intercession for us with groanings which cannot be uttered. And he that [searches] the hearts [knows] what is the mind of the Spirit, because he [makes] intercession for the saints according to the will of God.*

What kind of communication does the Holy Spirit use when He prompts us how to pray?

*Romans 8:26—But the Spirit itself [makes] intercession for us with **groanings which cannot be uttered**.*

When the Holy Spirit prays, He prays in us, and in so doing, He prompts us to pray. What does the Holy Spirit know and prompt us to pray?

*Romans 8:27—And he [God] that [searches] the hearts [knows] what is the mind of the Spirit, because He [the Holy Spirit makes] intercession for the saints according to the **will of God**.*

Throughout God's Word He communicated with men through a variety of methods. Sometimes He sent an angel. Once He spoke through a burning bush. He often used dreams. But two things were true about each instance of communication.

- The person knew it was God talking to him.

- He knew what God had said.

Scripture indicates that after God gave us the completed Bible, His revelation was complete; and we should no longer expect Him to continue using sensational signs to communicate with us. He continues to speak to our hearts and reveal His will through the Holy Spirit. Though we will not hear words, we can still expect the same two things to be true in His communication with us.

- We can know it is God communicating with us.

- We can know what He is saying.

22. How does God answer our prayers?

*Romans 8:32—He that spared not **his own Son**, but delivered him up for us all, how shall he not **with him** also **freely give us all things**?*

---

23. What does it mean to pray in Jesus' name?

*John 14:13–14—And whatsoever [you] shall ask **in my name**, that will I do, that the Father may be glorified in the Son. If [you] shall ask any thing **in my name**, I will do it.*

I often conclude my prayers by saying, "In Jesus' name I pray, Amen." This is not simply a formality of prayer but a recognition that the only ground I have to stand on in the throne room of God is the ground purchased for me by my exchanged life in Jesus. When we pray in Jesus' name, we are acknowledging our own unworthiness, and we are also claiming "Christ in us" as our right to call upon God.

If I go into a bank, show my identification, and ask for money, the teller will say to me, "I'm sorry. You have no money in this bank." If I take in a check made out to me and signed by one of their customers, it doesn't matter that I have no money in that bank. It matters only that the man who has signed the check has enough money to cover the check.

When we pray in Jesus' name, we are not hoping we have been good enough to merit God's favor so that He will answer our prayer. We come in the name of Jesus. He has promised to supply our every need, and He is good for the promise.

R. A. Torrey also taught, "Don't give up praying until you get what you are asking for, or until God makes it very clear that it is not His will to give it." How often do we get right up to the verge of a great blessing in prayer and just then let go? God often uses the time between our request and His answer to build our faith but only if we persist in prayer.

24. What did the Canaanite woman do to demonstrate she had great faith?

*Matthew 15:22–28—And, behold, a woman of Canaan came out of the same coasts, and **cried unto him** [Jesus], saying, Have mercy on me, O Lord, . . . Son of David; my daughter is grievously vexed with a devil. But he answered her not a word. And his disciples came and besought him, saying, Send her away; for **she [cries] after us**. But he answered and said, I am not sent but unto the lost sheep of the house of Israel. **Then came she and worshipped him, saying**, Lord, help me. But he answered and said, It is not meet to take the children's bread, and to cast it to dogs. **And she said**, Truth, Lord: yet the dogs eat of the crumbs which fall from their masters' table. Then Jesus answered and said unto her, O woman, great is [your] faith: be it unto [you] even as [you will]. And her daughter was made whole from that very hour.*

_____

25. If we persist in prayer, what does God promise He will do?

*Luke 18:1–8—And He [Jesus] spoke a parable unto them to this end, that men ought always to pray, and not to faint; Saying, There was in a city a judge, which feared not God, neither regarded man: and there was a widow in that city; and she came unto him, saying, Avenge me of mine adversary. And he would not for a while: but afterward he said within himself, Though I fear not God, nor regard man; yet because this widow [troubles] me, I will avenge her, lest by her continual coming she weary me. And the Lord said, Hear what the unjust judge [said]. And shall not God avenge **his own elect, which cry day and night unto him**, though he bear long with them? I tell you that **he will avenge them speedily**. Nevertheless when the Son of man [comes], shall he find **faith** on the earth?*

_____

When Jesus comes back to earth, what will He be looking for from His children?

_____

By praying for our needs and persisting in prayer, we demonstrate our faith.

HINDRANCES TO PRAYER

We have all these promises about praying, persisting, and always receiving. Then why aren't we seeing more of our prayers answered?

26. What missing ingredient leads to unanswered prayer?

*James 1:6–7—But let him **ask in faith**, nothing wavering. For **he that [wavers]** is like a wave of the sea driven with the wind and tossed. For **let not that man think that he shall receive** any thing of the Lord.*

_____

27. Why was God not answering the prayers of these people?

    *Ezekiel 14:3—Son of man, these men have set up their **idols in their heart**, and put **the stumblingblock of their iniquity** before their face: should I be enquired of at all by them?*

    _____

    What are some idols of the heart people have today?

    _____

    _____

28. Why does God say He doesn't give people what they desire?

    *James 4:2—You . . . desire to have, and cannot obtain: [you] fight and war, yet [you] have not, **because [you] ask not**.*

    _____

    When the same people did pray, why weren't their prayers answered?

    *James 4:3—[You] ask, and receive not, because [you] **ask amiss, that [you] may consume it upon your lusts**.*

    _____

29. The way we live can affect our prayer life. What is the hindrance to prayer in this verse?

    *1 Peter 3:7—Likewise, **husbands**, dwell with them according to knowledge, **giving honour unto the wife**, as unto the weaker vessel, and as being heirs together of the grace of life; **that your prayers be not hindered**.*

    _____

30. What did the psalmist know would hinder his prayers?

    *Psalm 66:18—If I **regard iniquity** in my heart, the Lord will not hear me.*

    _____

31. Is anyone sinless?

    1 John 1:8—If we say that we have no sin, we deceive ourselves, and the truth is not in us.

    _____

Look at number 30 again. It is **regarded sin** that is sure to hinder your walk with God and keep Him from answering your prayers. Remember what causes God to resist a man? **Pride.**

James 4:6—God [resists] the proud, but [gives] grace unto the humble.

If you have unconfessed sin in your life, won't you humble yourself right now before God and get right with Him? We must have grace. We can't function in our daily walk, let alone our prayer life, without it.

A PRACTICAL METHOD OF PRAYER

Evangelist Steve Pettit has developed this simple pattern of prayer to help you pray thirty minutes a day.

Praise (10 minutes)

Repent (5 minutes)

Ask (10 minutes)

Yield (5 minutes)

ASSIGNMENTS

Bible Reading: Acts 8–14

Scripture Memory:

> *Philippians 4:6–7—Be careful for nothing; but in every thing by prayer and supplication with thanksgiving let your requests be made known unto God. And the peace of God, which [passes] all understanding, shall keep your hearts and minds through Christ Jesus.*

(This verse is part of *The Exchange* Scripture Memory System.)

Practical Assignment: On a separate sheet of paper write a template for your prayer list and begin recording the requests the Lord lays on your heart this week. (You may want to buy a book to use as a prayer journal.)

If you have trouble making a list, ask your Bible study leader to help you.

Begin keeping track of the prayers you have seen answered. It will be a great blessing and source of joy in your life! It will also motivate you to keep praying for the rest of the things on your list.

Our God is a prayer-answering God!

LESSON 10

THE HOLY SPIRIT AND MY HOME LIFE

HOW TO LIVE AS A SPIRIT-FILLED MEMBER OF MY FAMILY

What comes to mind when you think of home? Mom? Apple pie? Front porch? Tension? Bickering? Broken promises? Shattered dreams? We all approach this subject from our own experiences—good or bad. The goal of this lesson is to look at God's ideal and make a plan to move our experience toward His ideal. Victory for this part of your life is also included in your inheritance rights in Christ.

A DESCRIPTION OF THE HOME

If becoming God's child changes anything in our lives for the better, it ought to change our relationship with our own families! Second Corinthians 2:14 teaches that God puts His victory on parade in the Christian's life. He wants to show the world Who He is through your life, and the place He wants to begin is in your home.

1. How is being Spirit-filled compared to being drunk?

   Ephesians 5:18—And be not drunk with wine, wherein is excess; but be filled with the Spirit.

   _____

Being Spirit-filled is allowing the Holy Spirit to control our every thought and action. Ephesians 5:19–6:10 deals with key areas of our lives that will be affected by the filling of the Holy Spirit. The vast majority of that section teaches how the Holy Spirit influences our relationships within our immediate families. God is an intimate friend Who desires to help us in our intimate relationships.

2. Who created the home?

   *Genesis 2:22–24—And the rib, which **the Lord God** had taken from man, made he a woman, and **brought her unto the man**. And Adam said, This is now bone of my bones, and flesh of my flesh: she shall be called Woman, because she was taken out of Man. Therefore shall a man leave his father and his mother, and shall cleave unto his wife: and they shall be one flesh.*

   _____

God brought Eve to Adam, and in the sinless environment before the fall of man, He created marriage. This unique phrase, "shall cleave unto his wife and they shall be one flesh," is found in only three other passages of the Bible—twice in the teachings of Jesus (Matthew 19:4–6; Mark 10:6–9) and once in the Ephesians 5 passage on the home.

The definition of marriage is widely debated in our culture, but from these four passages we derive six basic ingredients of marriage as God designed it.

THE SIX BIBLICAL INGREDIENTS OF MARRIAGE

- The establishment of a new family group distinct from parental relationships—"For this cause shall a man leave his father and mother." (Mark 10:7)

- The willful decision to join two lives into a binding relationship—"And cleave [glue] to his wife" (Mark 10:7)

- The permanent blending of two entities into one for the duration of life—"And they twain shall be one flesh: so then they are no more twain, but one flesh" (Mark 10:8)

- The initiation of an ongoing physical relationship given by the creator God exercised only within the confines of this unique relationship—*One flesh* includes physical intimacy (1 Corinthians 6:16; 7:1–5)

- The authorization of the marriage from God—"What therefore God [has] joined together" (Mark 10:9)

- The accountability of the marriage from man—"Let not man put asunder" (Mark 10:9)

Marriage is a covenant relationship in which one man and one woman vow before God in the presence of human witnesses to be faithful to an exclusive partnership that encompasses every area of life for the entire duration of life.

3. What truth did Jesus add to the phrase "shall cleave unto his wife and they shall be one flesh"?

Matthew 19:4–6—And he [Jesus] answered and said unto them, Have [you] not read, that he which made them at the beginning made them male and female, and said, For this cause shall a man leave father and mother, and shall cleave to his wife: and they twain shall be one flesh? Wherefore they are no more twain, but one flesh. **What therefore God [has] joined together, let not man put asunder.**

_____

Mark 10:6–9—But from the beginning of the creation God made them male and female. For this cause shall a man leave his father and mother, and cleave to his wife; and they twain shall be one flesh: so then they are no more twain, but one flesh. **What therefore God [has] joined together, let not man put asunder.**

_____

In Genesis 2 before man sinned, it was not necessary for God to teach us not to leave our marriages. All the unkindness and iniquities found in marriages today are due to man's sinful condition. Remember, Christ's exchange with you has given you the freedom to live His life of victory over sin and its effects. He wants to give you a marriage that exemplifies the fruit of the Holy Spirit—love, joy, peace, longsuffering, gentleness, goodness, faith, meekness, and temperance (Galatians 5:22–23).

What is added to the definition of marriage found in this passage dealing with Spirit-filled living in our homes?

Ephesians 5:31–32—For this cause shall a man leave his father and mother, and shall be joined unto his wife, and they two shall be one flesh. **This is a great mystery: but I speak concerning Christ and the church.**

_____

The marriage of Christ to the church is a real event that is going to take place in heaven. Many think of heaven as a distant, mystical place, far from their minds.

4. Does God want heaven to be far from our minds?

   *Colossians 3:2—**Set your affection on things above**, not on things on the earth.*

   _____

God wants us to have an eternal perspective in each area of life. In fact, He wants to illustrate heaven to others living here on earth through the earthly marriages of His children. You have probably heard the phrase "a little bit of heaven here on earth." This is what God had in mind when he designed the home.

5. What is the key to building a successful home?

   *Psalm 127:1—**Except the Lord build the house**, they labour in vain that build it: except the Lord keep the city, the watchman [wakes] but in vain.*

   _____

ROLES IN THE HOME

If you are to succeed in making your home the refuge and place of beauty God wants it to be, you must have the ingredients God prescribes for godly marriages.

The first ingredient for a godly marriage is a godly husband.

HUSBAND

6. Who has authority over the husband?

   *1 Corinthians 11:3—But I would have you know, that **the head of every man is Christ**; and the head of the woman is the man; and the head of Christ is God.*

   _____

7. What is the husband's role in the home?

   *Ephesians 5:23–24—For the **husband is the head** of the wife, even as Christ is the head of the church: and he is the saviour of the body. Therefore as the church is subject unto Christ, so let the wives be to their own husbands in every thing.*

   _____

8. What are husbands commanded to do?

   *Ephesians 5:25–29—**Husbands, love your wives**, even as Christ also loved the church, and gave himself for it; that he might sanctify and cleanse it with the washing of water by the word, that he might present it to himself a glorious church, not having spot, or wrinkle, or any such thing; but that it should be holy and without blemish. **So ought men to love their wives as their own bodies**. He that [loves] his wife [loves] himself. For no man ever yet hated his own flesh; but [nourishes] and [cherishes] it, even as the Lord the church.*

   _____

To what extent is the husband to love his wife?

Husbands, love your wives, even **as Christ also loved** *the church.*

_____

What does this kind of love demand?

Christ *also loved the church, and* **gave himself** *for it.*

_____

What motive should drive a godly husband?

*So ought men to love their wives as their own bodies. He that [loves] his wife [loves] himself. For no man ever yet hated his own flesh; but [**nourishes**] and [**cherishes**] it, even as the Lord the church.*

_____

The motive of a godly husband's love must be selfless, aimed at the edification and blessing of his wife.

What two verbs does God use to describe the love a godly husband should have for his wife? What do these words mean to you?

_____

_____

9. In Proverbs 5:15–21 God describes His plan for intimacy within the marriage. Look this up in your Bible and read it. In the middle of the passage He gives these commands:

    Proverbs 5:18—Rejoice with the wife of your youth.

    Proverbs 5:19—Be ravished always with her love.

    Do these commands demand a decision? What is it?

    _____

10. The Song of Solomon is an entire book of the Old Testament devoted to intimacy in marriage. How does this husband verbalize his choice to delight in his wife?

    Song of Solomon 4:9—[You have] ravished my heart, my sister, my spouse; [you have] ravished my heart with one of [your] eyes, with one chain of [your] neck.

    _____

11. What does it mean for a husband to live with his wife according to knowledge?

    1 Peter 3:7—Husbands, dwell with them according to knowledge, giving honour unto the wife, as unto the weaker vessel, and as being heirs together of the grace of life; that your prayers be not hindered.

    _____

In what ways can a husband honor his wife?

_____

Describe the significance of being equal heirs of our inheritance in Christ.

_____

Malachi 2:14 speaks of the wife of your youth, your companion, and the wife of your covenant. A godly husband must choose to cherish and delight in his wife, counting her as precious. When a husband lives this way, he creates "a little bit of heaven on earth" in his home. A wife who experiences this kind of love from her husband will not be afraid to fulfill her God-given role in the home.

The second ingredient of a godly marriage is a godly wife.

WIFE

12. Who has the authority over the wife?

    *Ephesians 5:23—For **the husband is the head of the wife**, even as Christ is the head of the church: and he is the saviour of the body.*

    _____

Remember who has authority over the husband. When a wife chooses to live under her husband's authority, she is living under God's authority.

13. What are wives commanded to do?

    *Ephesians 5:22—**Wives, submit yourselves** unto your own husbands, as unto the Lord.*

    _____

14. Why did God create a wife for Adam?

    *Genesis 2:18—And the Lord God said, It is not good that the man should be alone; I will **make him an help meet for him**.*

    _____

The word *meet* means "suitable," or "one that fits his needs." Eve was given to Adam as a helper who was made especially for him to meet his specific needs. Another way of understanding Eve's role is that she was created as Adam's completer. God ended every day of creation by pronouncing each thing he made as good. When God made Adam He said, "It is not good for a man to be alone." This is the first time God said something was not good. This was before sin. Adam was not complete without Eve. God made her as the completion of the team. Submission in marriage is a wife choosing to join her husband's team. She chooses to attach herself to him with the selfless motive of helping him make a home that is their "little bit of heaven on earth."

15. We have already seen that a husband is to love his wife and consider her precious. What is the wife's corresponding choice?

    *Ephesians 5:33—Nevertheless let every one of you in particular so love his wife even as himself; and the wife see that she **reverence [respect]** her husband.*

    _____

It is interesting that God never commands a wife to love her husband. This implies that love is more natural to a woman. Women need love to satisfy their heart's longing. This is why it is so important for a godly husband to love his wife. She is a responder; and when he fills her up with his love, it will be very natural for her to love him in return.

God's command for wives to respect their husbands is not natural for most women. God made man to need respect and gave him a wife to satisfy this need. Respect carries with it the idea of believing in him to the point of cheering him on. He needs to hear her appreciation of him.

16. What special promise does God give to a woman who is married to an unsaved husband?

    *1 Peter 3:1–6—Wives, be in subjection to your own husbands; that, if any obey not the word, **they** also **may without the word be won** by the conversation [lifestyle] of the wives; while they behold your chaste conversation coupled with fear. Whose adorning let it not be that outward adorning of plaiting the hair, and of wearing of gold, or of putting on of apparel; but let it be the hidden man of the heart, in that which is not corruptible, even the ornament of a meek and quiet spirit, which is in the sight of God of great price. For after this manner in the old time the holy women also, who trusted in God, adorned themselves, being in subjection unto their own husbands: even as Sara obeyed Abraham, calling him lord: whose daughters [you] are, as long as [you] do well, and are not afraid with any amazement.*

    _____

What outward evidence of the Spirit's filling will begin to win an unsaved husband to Christ?

*While they behold your chaste **[holy]** conversation **[lifestyle] coupled with** fear **[respect]**.*

_____

What must be her focus to ensure that he sees this holiness and respect from her?

***Whose adorning** let it not be that outward adorning of plaiting the hair, and of wearing of gold, or of putting on of apparel; but **let it be the hidden man of the heart**, in that which is not corruptible, even **the ornament of a meek and quiet spirit**, which is in the sight of God of great price.*

_____

What examples does God give of this kind of life?

*For after this manner in the old time the holy women also, who trusted in God, adorned themselves, being in subjection unto their own husbands: even as **Sara** obeyed Abraham.*

_____

In whom was their ultimate confidence?

Holy women also, who **trusted in God**

_____

Why did Sarah call her husband lord?

_____

The word *fear* and the word *lord* are words from an earlier time that in this verse carry the idea of respect. Frankly, respect is almost lost in our culture, but it is a vital ingredient in a godly home.

17. List at least five things you respect about your husband.

_____

_____

_____

Why don't you plan an appropriate time to express these specific areas of respect to him? You may be surprised at how much it pleases him. God made him to need this from you. You may underestimate the power you have in your relationship. If you become an expert in meeting this uniquely masculine need, your relationship will be revitalized with real intimacy and strength. He will be blessed and, in turn, you will be too.

No husband or wife can love or respect as God has planned unless the relationship with his or her spouse flows out of the relationship with God. One way I evaluate my relationship with God is by noticing how I am relating to my wife. If I am easily giving, expecting nothing in return, I know that I am experiencing God's abundant provision in my life to the point that I have plenty of overflow. If I am easily frustrated or am trying to manipulate and control her to do what I want her to do, then I know that I am walking in the flesh and can soon expect trouble in our relationship. I must constantly remind myself

> *My primary relationship with God is a receiving relationship.*
> *My primary relationship with others is a giving relationship.*

Only when I surrender to God and look to Him alone to meet all my needs do I have the desire and ability to give to others. One benefit of a close relationship is that it indicates, good or bad, my personal spiritual health. Selfish responses indicate that I have forgotten to see God as my sovereign provider and have begun to expect that provision from my loved one. Most of us want to focus on changing our spouse. Don't do that. Number one, it is impossible; and number two, it will drive him or her crazy. ***The only person you have the ability to change is yourself.*** One of my greatest confidences is the Christian's ability to change. The Holy Spirit is our change agent. Focus on Christ and ask Him to make you the husband or wife your spouse needs.

The third ingredient of a godly home is godly children. It is not necessary to have children to have a godly home; but if there are children in your home, they must be godly if you are to continue growing toward God's ideal for a Christian home.

CHILDREN

18. How does the Bible describe children?

   *Psalm 127:3—Lo, **children are an heritage [gift] of the Lord**: and the fruit of the womb is his reward.*

   _____

19. What are children commanded to do?

   *Ephesians 6:1–3—**Children, obey your parents** in the Lord: for this is right. **Honour your father and mother;** (which is the first commandment with promise;) that it may be well with [you], and [you] may live long on the earth.*

   _____

20. From this passage about loyalty and faithfulness in marriage, why does God give us children?

   *Malachi 2:15—And did not he make one? Yet had he the residue of the spirit. And wherefore one? **That he might seek a godly seed.** Therefore take heed to your spirit, and let none deal treacherously against the wife of his youth.*

   _____

21. How can parents raise godly children?

   *Proverbs 22:6—**Train up a child in the way he should go**: and when he is old, he will not depart from it.*

   _____

BIBLICAL TRAINING

22. As the head of his family, what is a godly father commanded not to do?

   Ephesians 6:4—And, [you] fathers, provoke not your children to wrath: but bring them up in the nurture and admonition of the Lord.

   _____

   What is he commanded to do?

   Bring them up in the _____ and _____ of the Lord.

Obviously this is a two-parent job as a wife joins her husband to build a godly home working side by side with him to train up godly children. The word *nurture* carries with it the idea of training or discipline. A great picture of this process is a soldier in training for deployment. He is trained in a controlled, safe environment so that he will be ready to face an uncontrolled, hostile battlefield. A godly home is like a greenhouse. It provides the nutrients and warm environment needed to prepare godly children for a cold, harsh world. The word *discipline* does not simply refer to punishment when a child has done wrong It is the process of discipling a child to be strong and prepared to face the world as a young adult. This process is designed to build character into the fabric of the child and demands hard work and a disciplined lifestyle.

The word *admonition* can literally be translated "to set the mind," like setting the table for dinner. You put everything in place and get it ready for use. The training of a godly mind includes filling the moral warehouse of the child. When a child has been properly trained in biblical distinctions of right and wrong, his conscience is prepared to continue disciplining him when he grows to maturity and independence.

23. How would you describe biblical chastisement?

   *Proverbs 13:24—He that [spares] his rod [hates] his son: but he that [loves] him **[chastens] him betimes [early]**.*

   _____

24. What is the result of loving chastisement?

   *Proverbs 22:15—Foolishness **[rebellion]** is bound in the heart of a child; but the rod of correction shall **drive it far from him**.*

   _____

25. What is the spiritual result of chastisement?

   *Proverbs 23:13–14—Withhold not correction from the child: for if [you beat] him with the rod, he shall not die. [You shall] beat him with the rod, and [shall] **deliver his soul from hell**.*

   _____

These words seem harsh, but the message is simple and clear. Appropriate corporal punishment is part of God's prescription for raising godly children. God is our example of a loving Father, and He is never angry or abusive in His chastisement. He is firm and consistent in dealing with His children.

26. Who does God not chastise?

   *Hebrews 12:5–8—My son, despise not . . . the chastening of the Lord, nor faint when [you are] rebuked of him: for whom the Lord [loves] he [chastens], and [scourges] every son whom he [receives]. If [you] endure chastening, God [deals] with you as with sons; for what son is he whom the father [chastens] not? But if [you] be without chastisement, whereof all are partakers, then are [you] bastards **[not true children], and not sons**.*

   _____

God designed loving chastisement to be an effective tool in godly parenting. He calls it an act of love, and it is certainly not to be applied out of anger. He planned for it to be combined with other forms of discipline: godly instruction, encouragement, and the building of loving, trusting relationships. All this must flow from a Spirit-filled Christian. In essence, God wants to raise your children through you. He is their Father and is using you to show them His love and lead them to place their trust in Him.

FAMILY DEVOTIONS

27. What are we to teach our children?

   *Deuteronomy 6:6–7—And **these words**, which I command [you] this day, shall be in [your] heart: and [you shall] **teach them diligently unto [your] children**, and shall talk of them when [you sit in your] house, and when [you walk] by the way, and when [you lie] down, and when [you rise] up.*

   _____

*2 Timothy 3:15–16—And that from a child [you have] known the **holy scriptures**, which are able to make [you] wise unto salvation through faith which is in Christ Jesus. All Scripture is given by inspiration of God, and is profitable for doctrine, for reproof, for correction, for instruction in righteousness.*

_____

28. Who should lead the home in godly instruction?

*Genesis 18:18–19—Seeing that Abraham shall surely become a great and mighty nation, and all the nations of the earth shall be blessed in him? For I know him, that **he will command his children and his household after him, and they shall keep the way of the Lord**, to do justice and judgment.*

_____

*Genesis 35:2–3—Then **Jacob said unto his household**, and to all that were with him, Put away the strange gods that are among you, and be clean, and change your garments: and let us arise, and go up to Bethel; and I will make there an altar unto God.*

_____

*Joshua 24:15—And if it seem evil unto you to serve the Lord, choose you this day whom [you] will serve; whether the gods which your fathers served that were on the other side of the flood, or the gods of the Amorites, in whose land [you] dwell: but **as for me and my house, we will serve the Lord**.*

_____

Through the years, godly husbands and fathers have led their families in a time of Bible instruction and prayer. It may take only a few minutes every day, but it sets a precedent in your home as Joshua did in his. You are saying, "As for me and my house, we will serve the Lord!" The example a man sets for his children and the accountability he keeps with his wife are essential. One of the most important ingredients of a godly home is a daily time of family devotions.

THE SACREDNESS OF THE HOME

God designed the home to show His love and care for His children and their loyalty and devotion to Him. Our home can only become this picture of heaven on earth as we walk in the power and victory of the Holy Spirit. I once talked to a wife about her husband who said something that was a little alarming to me when she first said it. She told me that living with her husband was "like living with Jesus." She was not being sacrilegious; she was experiencing a husband who was living the Spirit-filled life.

29. Remember who Paul said was living in him?

*Galatians 2:20—I am crucified with Christ: nevertheless I live; yet not I, but **Christ [lives] in me**.*

_____

Paul was living the Christ-life. The Spirit of Christ was controlling his thoughts and actions. Jesus wants to live through you in your home. We sing a song in our church entitled "Heaven Came Down and Glory Filled My Soul." This is how we build homes that are "a little bit of heaven on earth." The day we got saved, God put His Holy Spirit in our lives as down payment for heaven. When He is producing His fruit in our lives, the first people who will experience the difference in our lives are those who live in our homes.

A great travesty in our culture is the destruction of our homes through divorce. In an argument between God and the Israelites recorded in the book of Malachi, God accused the nation of dealing treacherously, committing abominations, and profaning the holiness of the Lord. He also accused them of covering His altar with tears and weeping and wailing to the point that He no longer heard their prayers. Malachi records the climax of the argument:

Malachi 2:14—Yet [you] say, Wherefore? Because the Lord has been witness between [you] and the wife of [your] youth, against whom [you have] dealt treacherously: yet she is [your] companion, and the wife of [your] covenant.

30. How does God view divorce?

*Malachi 2:15–16—Take heed to your spirit, and let none deal treacherously against the wife of his youth. For **the Lord, the God of Israel**, [says] that he [**hates**] **putting away** [**divorce**]: for one [covers] violence with his garment, [says] the Lord of hosts: therefore take heed to your spirit, that [you] deal not treacherously.*

_____

31. Is divorce ever a biblical option?

*Mark 10:6–9—But from the beginning of the creation God made them male and female. For this cause shall a man leave his father and mother, and cleave to his wife; and they twain shall be one flesh: so then they are no more twain, but one flesh. **What therefore God [has] joined together, let not man put asunder**.*

_____

32. What did Christ say about those who remarry after a divorce?

*Matthew 19:9—And I say unto you, Whosoever shall put away his wife, except it be for fornication, and shall marry another, [**commits**] **adultery**: and whoso marries her which is put away [**commits**] **adultery**.*

_____

You can't change a divorce in your past, but you can confess it to God and get it right with Him. Determine to honor God's institution of marriage for the rest of your life. God doesn't want us to live in guilt. Once you have dealt with this, don't allow the Devil to continue beating you up with it. Use feelings of hurt or regret to fuel your zeal for the Lord today and in the future.

APPLICATION

James 1:22–25 promises God's special blessing on those who take action on what His Word teaches.

33. If your marriage is to be permanent, you must follow God's plan. What is *your* responsibility according to the Scriptures?

_____

_____

_____

_____

34. What will make your home a happier place?

_____

_____

_____

_____

_____

35. What areas of child rearing do you need to work on this week?

_____

_____

_____

_____

_____

_____

36. In what ways will you show that you are committed to your marriage?

_____

_____

_____

_____

_____

_____

_____

ASSIGNMENTS

Bible Reading: Acts 15–21

Scripture Memory:

Acts 16:31—And they said, Believe on the Lord Jesus Christ, and [you shall] be saved, and [your] house.

(This verse is part of *The Exchange* Scripture Memory System.)

Practical Assignment: Write a description of your God-given role in your home.

_____

_____

_____

_____

_____

Evaluate your effectiveness.

_____

_____

_____

_____

List areas you are willing to ask God to help you change.

_____

_____

_____

_____

Write one or more verses you can use to allow God to remind you and strengthen you toward these changes.

_____

_____

_____

_____

LESSON 11

THE HOLY SPIRIT AND MY FINANCIAL LIFE

HOW TO ADOPT GOD'S ATTITUDE TOWARD MY MONEY

As a Christian you will have a different attitude toward wealth than you had before you were saved. God has given us the privilege of living in and for His eternal kingdom. You have probably seen the bumper sticker that reads, "The one who dies with the most toys wins." I saw one recently that puts things into perspective. It read, "The one who dies with the most toys still dies." No matter what we are able to accumulate here on earth, we cannot take any of it with us; yet everything we do in and for the eternal kingdom of God will last forever. God teaches us that we are not owners of what we possess, but stewards. God owns everything and will ask us to give account of how we used what He allowed us to have while we were here on earth. He expects us to support His work and has promised to reward those who do. In this world of borrowing and acquiring more and more things, we must remind ourselves of the biblical injunctions regarding materialism. Study this lesson carefully and discover rich treasures in God's Word!

Psalm 119:72—The law of [Your] mouth is better unto me than thousands of gold and silver.

Psalm 119:127—Therefore I love [Your] commandments above gold; yea, above fine gold.

ETERNAL VERSUS TEMPORAL

1. What is the most valuable thing entrusted to you?

*Matthew 16:26—For what is a man profited, if he shall gain the whole world, and lose **his own soul**? or what shall a man give in exchange for **his soul**?*

_____

Jesus used these questions to sum up a rebuke He gave Simon Peter. The root of Peter's error was savoring the things of men instead of the things of God. Jesus then invited all the disciples to follow Him, telling them that such a decision would demand self-denial in this life but would yield eternal value in the life to come. He was talking about filling one's soul with the desires and values of the eternal kingdom of God versus the temporal things of this age. Even if we accumulate everything our soul desires, we will not be satisfied. Only filling our soul with the living Spirit of God gives real life and value.

2. In the parable of the rich fool, what happened to the man who pursued material wealth at the expense of his own soul?

*Luke 12:15–21—And he said unto them, Take heed, and **beware of covetousness**: for a man's life [consists] not in the abundance of the things which he [possesses]. And he [spoke] a parable unto them, saying, The ground of a certain rich man brought forth plentifully: and he thought within himself, saying, What shall I do, because I have no room where to bestow my fruits? And he said, This will I do: I will pull down my barns, and build greater; and there will I bestow all my fruits and my goods. And I will say to my soul, Soul, [you have] much goods laid up for many years; take [your] ease, eat, drink, and be merry. But God said unto him, [you] fool, **this night your soul shall be required of [you]**: then whose shall those things be, which [you have] provided? So is he that [lays] up treasure for himself, and is not rich toward God.*

_____

Read the first verse again. What lesson was Jesus trying to teach by this parable?

_____

How would you describe the word *covetousness*?

_____

Covetousness is wanting what God has not chosen to give you. It is a greedy desire for what we can't or shouldn't have. Why did Jesus say to beware of it?

_____

What contrast did Jesus make after He told the parable?

_____

Like most people in our culture, we can work to accumulate things or we can aim to be rich toward God. Which are you doing, and which is more valuable?

3. Will earthly riches equate to eternal riches?

Matthew 19:23–26—Then said Jesus unto his disciples, Verily I say unto you, That a rich man shall hardly enter into the kingdom of heaven. And again I say unto you, It is easier for a camel to go through the eye of a needle, than for a rich man to enter into the kingdom of God. When his disciples heard it, they were exceedingly amazed, saying, Who then can be saved? But Jesus beheld them, and said unto them, With men this is impossible; but with God all things are possible.

_____

4. What is the danger of working for the sole purpose of becoming rich?

*Proverbs 23:4–5—Labour not to be rich: cease from your own wisdom. Will you set [your] eyes upon that which is not? for **riches certainly make themselves wings; they fly away** as an eagle toward heaven.*

_____

5. Why does God tell us to focus on the invisible kingdom of God?

    *2 Corinthians 4:18—While we look not at the things which are seen, but at the things which are not seen: for the things which are seen are temporal; but the **things which are not seen are eternal**.*

    _____

Verses 4–7 of the same passage teach that the real treasure in this world is the light that Jesus brings into our life at salvation, and the pursuit that is genuinely valuable is introducing the world to "the light of the glorious gospel of Christ."

The Sermon on the Mount, the longest message Jesus preached, is recorded in the book of Matthew. A large portion of this important sermon dealt with His value system regarding treasures.

6. What are the reasons given for not working for temporal treasures but rather laboring tirelessly for eternal treasure?

    *Matthew 6:19–20—Lay not up for yourselves treasures upon earth, where **moth and rust . . . corrupt**, and where **thieves break through and steal**: But lay up for yourselves treasures in heaven, **where neither moth nor rust . . . corrupt, and where thieves do not break through nor steal**.*

    _____

7. What is the alarming truth concerning our treasure and our heart?

    Matthew 6:21—For where your treasure is, there will your heart be also.

    _____

We make a choice about where we are going to put our treasure, and our heart follows that choice. The next few verses warn us of the danger of trying to labor for both temporal and eternal treasure. We must choose which we will serve.

*Matthew 6:24—No man can serve two masters: for either he will hate the one, and love the other; or else he will hold to the one, and despise the other. **You cannot serve God and mammon** [earthly riches personified into a deity].*

8. He continues by teaching us not to center our lives on physical needs. What enables us to stop worrying about earthly needs?

    *Matthew 6:31–32—Therefore take no thought, saying, What shall we eat? or, What shall we drink? or, Wherewithal shall we be clothed? (For after **all these things** do the Gentiles seek:) for **your heavenly Father [knows] that [you] have need of all these things**.*

    _____

9. On what must we center our lives?

    *Matthew 6:33—But **seek . . . first the kingdom of God**, and his righteousness; and **all these things shall be added unto you**.*

    _____

What does Jesus promise when we put His invisible, eternal kingdom first in our lives?

_____

Notice the phrase "all these things." It is used three times in two verses. Things are important, even necessary, but not as important and necessary as Christ's kingdom. God knows we have only so much emotional energy to expend. If we expend our energy on earthly anxieties and desires, we will have none left for what is truly valuable. Jesus sums up the passage with this verse:

> *Matthew 6:34—Take therefore no thought for the morrow: for the morrow shall take thought for the things of itself. Sufficient unto the day is the evil thereof.*

STEWARDSHIP VERSUS OWNERSHIP

A sixteenth-century preacher described the difference between the temporal and the eternal this way: "When the possessor of Heaven and Earth brought you into being and placed you in this world, He placed you here not as an owner, but as a steward—as such He entrusted you for a season with goods of various kinds—but the sole property of these still rests in Him, nor can ever be alienated from Him. As you are not your own but His, such is likewise all you enjoy." We must learn to properly manage what the Lord places within our care.

10. Who is the real owner of all things?

> *Psalm 24:1—**The earth is the Lord's**, and the fulness thereof; the world, and they that dwell therein.*

_____

> *Psalm 50:10–12—For every beast of the forest is mine, and the cattle upon a thousand hills. I know all the fowls of the mountains: and the wild beasts of the field are mine. If I were hungry, I would not tell [you]: for **the world is mine**, and the fulness thereof.*

_____

Landowners in Bible times often had a steward to manage their estates. Servants were employed to run the day-to-day affairs of their properties and assets. The landowner would take account of the books only periodically. Jesus told a parable about an unjust steward who knew that such an accounting was coming. Because the property was not his own, he utilized his power over the use of those things to secure a good standing for himself so that when he was fired from his job, he would still have friends to draw from in his life after stewardship. While not condoning his dishonesty, Jesus commended his astuteness.

How does Jesus want us to utilize our power over the things He has entrusted to our care?

> *Luke 16:8–9—And the Lord commended the unjust steward, because he had done wisely: for the children of this world are in their generation wiser than the children of light. And I say unto you, **Make to yourselves friends of the mammon [money] of unrighteousness**; that, when [you] fail, they may receive you into everlasting habitations.*

_____

God wants you to use things to reach people for the kingdom of God instead of using people to acquire things.

11. What does God require of His stewards?

*1 Corinthians 4:2—Moreover it is required in stewards, that a man **be found faithful**.*

_____

Jesus told another parable of a master who was going away for a long time. He made three of his servants stewards over large sums of money called talents. Each talent was worth about fifteen years' wages, or $500,000–$700,000. He gave one five talents, another two talents, and to the last one talent.

12. List what each man did with his master's money and the master's response to each servant.

*Matthew 25:15–30—And unto one he gave five talents, to another two, and to another one; to every man according to his several ability; and straightway took his journey. Then **he that had received the five talents went and traded with the same, and made them other five talents**. And likewise **he that had received two, he also gained other two**. But **he that had received one went and dug in the earth, and hid his lord's money**. After a long time the lord of those servants [came], and [reckoned] with them. And so **he that had received five talents** came and brought other five talents, saying, Lord, [you delivered] unto me five talents: behold, I have gained beside them five talents more. His lord said unto him, **Well done . . . good and faithful servant**: [you have] been faithful over a few things, I will make [you] ruler over many things: enter . . . into the joy of [your] lord. **He also that had received two talents** came and said, Lord, [you delivered] unto me two talents: behold, I have gained two other talents beside them. His lord said unto him, **Well done, good and faithful servant**; [you have] been faithful over a few things, I will make [you] ruler over many things: enter . . . into the joy of [your] lord. Then **he which had received the one talent** came and said, lord, I knew [you] that [you are] an hard man, reaping where [you have] not sown, and gathering where [you have] not strawed: and I was afraid, and went and hid your talent in the earth: lo, there [you have] that is [yours]. His Lord answered and said unto him, **[You] wicked and slothful servant**, [you knew] that I reap where I sowed not, and gather where I have not strawed: [you ought] therefore to have put my money to the exchangers, and then at my coming I should have received mine own with usury. **Take therefore the talent from him**, and give it unto him which [has] ten talents. For unto every one that [has] shall be given, and **he shall have abundance**: but from him that [has] not shall be taken away even that which he [has]. And cast [you] the unprofitable servant into outer darkness: there shall be weeping and gnashing of teeth.*

The Five-Talent Servant

What he did:

_____

His master's response:

_____

The Two-Talent Servant

What he did:

_____

His master's response:

_____

The One-Talent Servant

What he did:

_____

His master's response:

_____

The abundance given as a reward to those who have invested their Lord's money wisely is no doubt a picture of the eternal reward given to those who invest their earthly stewardship into the invisible, eternal kingdom of God.

GIVING VERSUS GETTING

13. The very last words Paul spoke to the church leaders in Asia indicate the importance Paul placed on giving. Why does God want us to give?

    Acts 20:35—I have showed you all things, how that so labouring [you] ought to support the weak, and to remember the words of the Lord Jesus, how he said, **It is more blessed to give than to receive**.

    _____

14. What promise allows us to give generously?

    Philippians 4:19—**But my God shall supply all your need** according to his riches in glory by Christ Jesus.

    _____

15. What word describes the mindset God wants us to have?

    1 Timothy 6:6–8—But **godliness with contentment is great gain**. For we brought nothing into this world, and it is certain we can carry nothing out. And having food and raiment let us be therewith content.

    _____

16. Does the Bible say it is wrong to be rich?

    1 Timothy 6:9–10—But **they that will be rich** fall into temptation and a snare, and into many foolish and hurtful lusts, which drown men in destruction and perdition. For **the love of money** is the root of all evil: which while some coveted after, they have erred from the faith, and pierced themselves through with many sorrows.

    _____

    What is the root of every kind of evil?

    _____

Having money is not wrong; loving money is. In fact, God recognizes that some people are going to be wealthier than others and gives advice to help them best utilize their earthly assets.

17. How does the Bible describe riches?

    *1 Timothy 6:17–19—Charge them that are rich in this world, that they be not highminded, nor trust in **uncertain riches**, but in the living God, who [gives] us richly all things to enjoy; that they do good, that they be rich in good works, ready to distribute, willing to communicate; **laying up in store** for themselves **a good foundation** against the time to come, that they may lay hold on eternal life.*

    _____

    When we give of our earthly goods, what are we actually doing?

    _____

18. We live in a world that is always hungering for more. To what does the Bible equate this covetous mindset?

    *Ephesians 5:5—For this [you] know, that no whoremonger, nor unclean person, nor **covetous man, who is an idolater**, [has] any inheritance in the kingdom of Christ and of God.*

    _____

    *Colossians 3:5—Mortify therefore your members which are upon the earth; fornication, uncleanness, inordinate affection, evil concupiscence, and **covetousness, which is idolatry**.*

    _____

The right attitude about money is not possible without the Holy Spirit's control. Paul actually called the *giving* of the churches of Macedonia the grace of God.

19. What do you see that indicates Spirit-filled living in the lives of the Macedonian givers?

    *2 Corinthians 8:1–5—Moreover, brethren, we do you to wit [witness] of **the grace of God** bestowed on the churches of Macedonia; how that in a great trial of affliction the abundance of their joy and their deep poverty abounded unto the riches of their liberality. For to their power, I bear record, yea, and beyond their power they were willing of themselves; praying us with much entreaty that we would receive the gift, and take upon us the fellowship of the ministering to the saints. And this they did, not as we hoped, but **first gave their own selves to the Lord**, and unto us by the will of God.*

    _____

20. Who first demonstrated the grace of giving?

    *2 Corinthians 8:9—For [you] know **the grace of our Lord Jesus Christ**, that, though he was rich, yet for your sakes he became poor, that you through his poverty might be rich.*

    _____

    Notice the beauty of the exchange Christ made for us. Can you ever give more than Christ gave to you?

    _____

109

TITHING

The baseline for biblical giving is called tithing.

21.   What is the definition of the word *tithe*?

*Leviticus 27:32—And concerning the tithe of the herd, or of the flock, even of whatsoever passes under the rod, **the tenth shall be holy unto the Lord**.*

The first mention of any truth in the Bible often lays the foundation for the expansion of that truth throughout the rest of the Bible. This is true of the first mention of tithing recorded in Genesis 14:17–24. Abraham gave tithes of the spoil of battle to Melchizedek, who was a type of Christ.

22.   In your opinion, why did Abraham give Melchizedek a tithe?

*Genesis 14:19–20—And he [Melchizedek] blessed him, and said, **Blessed be Abram of the most high God, possessor of heaven and earth**: and blessed be the most high God, which [has] delivered thine enemies into thy hand. And he gave him tithes of all.*

---

23.   What reason did Abraham give for refusing money from the wicked king of Sodom?

*Genesis 14:22—And Abram said to the king of Sodom, **I have lift up mine hand unto the Lord, the most high God, the possessor of heaven and earth**.*

Because Abraham recognized that he had been blessed with success by God, he was giving a portion of the blessing back to God to acknowledge that everything he possessed had come from God. The phrase "I have lift up mine hand" signified a covenant made with God. As you invest your money in the Lord's work, you make a statement about your own personal relationship with God, acknowledging His ownership of everything you have.

24.   What sin did God accuse His people of committing when they refused to tithe?

*Malachi 3:8—**Will a man rob God?** Yet [you] have robbed me. But [you] say, Wherein have we robbed [You]? In tithes and offerings.*

---

25.   How does God challenge His children to tithe?

*Malachi 3:10—Bring . . . all the tithes into the storehouse, that there may be meat in mine house, and **prove me now** herewith, says the Lord of hosts, **if I will not open you the windows of heaven, and pour you out a blessing**, that there shall not be room enough to receive it.*

God's plan for caring for the house of God is that all His people give generously to His work. If each church member were to give a baseline 10 percent of his income to his local church, the church would be able to invest far more in God's eternal, invisible kingdom. According to a recent Barna Research report, only "9% of born again Christians tithed their income to churches in 2004" (www.barna.org). By our disobedience we are missing great spiritual blessing from God.

26.   What promise does God give to those who are obedient in their giving?

*Luke 6:38—**Give, and it shall be given unto you**; good measure, pressed down, and shaken together, and running over, shall men give into your bosom. For with the same measure that [you] mete withal it shall be measured to you again.*

_____

The inheritance Christ has given us is a spiritual one. Though these verses do not promise health and wealth physically, they do promise spiritual health and wealth, which is far more valuable.

27.   What attitude does God desire from those who give?

*2 Corinthians 9:6–7—But this I say, He which [sows] sparingly shall reap also sparingly; and he which [sows] bountifully shall reap also bountifully. Every man according as he [purposes] in his heart, so let him give; not grudgingly, or of necessity: for **God [loves] a cheerful giver**.*

_____

28.   When should you give your tithes and offerings?

*1 Corinthians 16:1–2—Now concerning the collection for the saints, as I have given order to the churches of Galatia, even so do [you]. **Upon the first day of the week** let every one of you lay by him in store, **as God [has] prospered him**, that there be no gatherings when I come.*

_____

What is the standard of giving mentioned here?

_____

The Bible directs us to regular, purposeful giving in proportion to His provision. God's reward to the five-talent servant and the two-talent servant was the same.

God rewards faithful stewardship.

SAVING VERSUS BORROWING

"The total amount of consumer [unsecured] debt in the United States stands at nearly $2.6 trillion dollars—and based on the latest Census statistics, that works out to be nearly $8,500 in debt for every man, woman and child that lives in the US." This is not counting mortgages. This is $34,000 of consumer debt for an average family of four. "The size of the total consumer debt grew nearly five times in size from 1980 ($355 billion) to 2001 ($1.7 trillion)." "Nearly one in every 35 households in the United States filed for bankruptcy in 2007" (www.money-zine.com). We live in a "buy now pay later" culture, but the Bible doesn't promote this lifestyle.

29. What does the Bible teach concerning debt?

    Proverbs 22:7—The borrower is servant to the lender.

    _____

30. What does the Bible call people who don't repay their debts?

    *Psalm 37:21—The **wicked** [borrows], and [pays] not again: but the righteous [shows] mercy, and [gives].*

    _____

31. What are the items for which the people in this story borrowed money? What was the result of their actions?

    *Nehemiah 5:3–5—Some also there were that said, We have mortgaged our lands, vineyards, and houses, that **we might buy corn**, because of the dearth. There were also that said, We have borrowed money for **the king's tribute**, and that upon our lands and vineyards. Yet now our flesh is as the flesh of our brethren, our children as their children: and, lo, we bring into bondage our sons and our daughters to be servants, and some of our daughters are brought unto bondage already: **neither is it in our power to redeem them**; for other men have our lands and vineyards.*

    _____

This passage does not teach against borrowing, but it certainly demonstrates that borrowing to get out of trouble makes a bad situation worse. The Bible promotes a "pay as you go and save for the future" lifestyle.

32. What words does God use to describe those who save?

    *Proverbs 15:6—In the house of the **righteous** is much treasure: but in the revenues of the wicked is trouble.*

    *Proverbs 21:20—There is treasure to be desired and oil in the dwelling of the **wise**; but **a foolish man [spends] it up**.*

    _____

    How does God describe those who do not save?

    _____

33. What is a motive to save as much as you can?

    *Proverbs 19:14—**House and riches are the inheritance** of fathers: and a prudent wife is from the Lord.*

    *Proverbs 13:22—**A good man [leaves] an inheritance** to his children's children: and the wealth of the sinner is laid up for the just.*

    _____

The Bible also promotes a strong work ethic. One of the Ten Commandments teaches the importance of long days and long weeks of hard labor. While rest is necessary it is not the objective. We rest so that we have the energy to work, not work so that we have the time to rest.

Exodus 20:9–10—Six days [shall you] labour, and do all [your] work: but the seventh day is the sabbath of the Lord [your] God: in it [you shall] not do any work.

34. What is the priority taught in this verse?

    *Proverbs 24:27—Prepare **your work** without, and make it fit for [yourself] in the field; and afterwards build [your] house.*

    _____

35. What does the Bible teach should happen to people who won't work?

    *2 Thessalonians 3:10—For even when we were with you, this we commanded you, that if any would not work, **neither should he eat**.*

    _____

36. What does this verse teach about hard work?

    *Ephesians 4:28—Let him that stole steal no more: but rather **let him labour, working with his hands** the thing which is good, **that he may have to give** to him that [needs].*

    _____

From contentment to over-borrowing, and from working to giving, God has shown us what to do. The Holy Spirit of God will enable us to make the changes necessary to do it.

Romans 11:36—For of him, and through him, and to him, are all things: to whom be glory for ever. Amen.

Philippians 2:13—For it is God which [works] in you both to will and to do of his good pleasure.

APPLICATION

James 1:22–25 promises God's special blessing on those who take action on what His Word teaches. What will you do as a result of what you have learned from God's Word?

_____

_____

_____

_____

_____

ASSIGNMENTS

Bible Reading: Acts 22–28

Scripture Memory:

> *Matthew 6:33—But seek . . . first the kingdom of God, and his righteousness; and all these things shall be added unto you.*

(This verse is part of *The Exchange* Scripture Memory System.)

Practical Assignment: Answer the following questions. If you are married, talk with your spouse about your responses.

Based on the Word of God, have you been tithing on a regular basis?   Yes   No

Are you giving to the work of the Lord above the tithe?   Yes   No

Have you prayed about what the Lord would have you do concerning missions giving?   Yes   No

Do you feel that you have a joyful spirit toward your giving?   Yes   No

Would you say that both your treasure and your heart are indeed in heaven?   Yes   No

Ask the Lord to show you areas of your finances He would like to change. Write down what He brings to mind.

_____

_____

_____

_____

_____

LESSON 12

THE FRUITFULNESS OF MY SERVICE

FULFILLING THE PURPOSE OF THE SPIRIT-FILLED LIFE— SERVICE FOR THE KING

The purpose of the Spirit-filled life is to manifest, or demonstrate, Christ to the world around us. God doesn't fill us so that we can be full and satisfied. He fills us so that He can pour His life into the world through us. The most exciting truth in the world is who we are in Christ. Each of us is a new creation. God has filled us with the victory of Jesus and enabled us to live that victory in the face of every imaginable opposition. Paul uses Romans 8:37 to answer the question of what might defeat us. "Nay, in all these things **we are more than conquerors through him** that loved us." Now that we have this victorious power from God, He plans for us to use that power to serve in His eternal, invisible kingdom.

THE ENABLING

1. What is the purpose for God's grace?

    *2 Corinthians 9:8—And God is able to make all grace abound toward you; **that [you]**, always having all sufficiency in all things, **may abound to every good work**.*

    _____

    *Ephesians 2:8–10—For by grace are [you] saved through faith; and that not of yourselves: it is the gift of God: not of works, lest any man should boast. For **we are his workmanship, created in Christ Jesus unto good works**, which God [has] before ordained that we should walk in them.*

    _____

2. Grace is God's supernatural enablement to do what only God can do. What good work was Paul energized by God's grace to do?

    *Ephesians 3:7–8—Whereof I was made a minister, according to the gift of the grace of God given unto me by the effectual working of his power. Unto me, who am less than the least of all saints, is this grace given, **that I should preach** among the Gentiles **the unsearchable riches of Christ**.*

    _____

3. In the following verse, as in Galatians 2:20, Paul used the phrase "yet not I" to describe the supernatural ability to live as he did. What was Paul able to do that the phrase "yet not I" describes?

*1 Corinthians 15:10–11—**By the grace of God** I am what I am: and his grace which was bestowed upon me was not in vain; but **I laboured more abundantly** than they all: yet not I, but the grace of God which was with me. Therefore whether it were I or they, so **we preach**, and so **you believed**.*

THE CALL

Aren't you glad you got saved? Think back to the day you accepted Christ. What did it take for you to become a Christian? Obviously, salvation is from God, but it probably took a person to explain God's Word to you, to show you how to receive Christ's exchange. Now that you are saved, you have the privilege and responsibility to tell others the Good News!

4. Even Jesus lived in dependence on the Holy Spirit. What did the Holy Spirit anoint Him to do during His earthly ministry?

*Luke 4:18—The Spirit of the Lord is upon me, because **he [has] anointed me to preach the gospel to the poor**; he [has] sent me **to heal the brokenhearted, to preach deliverance** to the captives, and **recovering of sight** to the blind, to **set at liberty** them that are bruised.*

5. What did Jesus promise those who follow Him?

*Matthew 4:19—And he said unto them, Follow me, and **I will make you fishers of men**.*

6. What was His final command to the disciples? Do you remember what this command is called?

*Mark 16:15—And he said unto them, Go . . . into all the world, and **preach the gospel to every creature**.*

7. Can anyone be saved? _____ What must happen before someone can be saved?

*Romans 10:13–15—For whosoever shall call upon the name of the Lord shall be saved. How then shall they call on him in whom they have not believed? and how shall they believe in him of whom they have not heard? and **how shall they hear without a preacher**? And how shall they preach, except they be sent? as it is written, **How beautiful are the feet of them that preach the gospel of peace**, and bring glad tidings of good things!*

The word *preacher* does not indicate a professional but anyone who proclaims the gospel of peace.

How does God view those who broadcast His good news?

8. What has Jesus ordained for you to do?

    *John 15:16—[You] have not chosen me, **but I have chosen you**, and ordained you, **that [you] should go and bring forth fruit**, and that your fruit should remain: that whatsoever [you] shall ask of the Father in my name, he may give it you.*

9. Earlier in this discourse Jesus told His disciples what they needed to be equipped to be a fruitful Christian. What was it?

    *John 15:4–5—**Abide in me**, and I **in you**. As the branch cannot bear fruit of itself, except it abide in the vine; no more can [you], except [you] abide in me. I am the vine, [you] are the branches: he that [abides] in me, and I in him, **the same [brings] forth much fruit**: for without me [you] can do nothing.*

THE BOLDNESS

10. How did spending time with Jesus change the disciples' ministry after His ascension?

    *Acts 4:13—Now when they [the rulers] saw **the boldness of Peter and John**, and perceived that they were unlearned and ignorant men, they marvelled; and they took knowledge of them, that **they had been with Jesus**.*

This boldness became a trademark of Jesus' followers. Knowing Jesus intimately gives us the ability to *show* Him boldly to others. Shortly after this incident the disciples were threatened never to "speak at all nor teach in the name of Jesus" again. Even though they were released under close scrutiny, they went immediately to where the church was meeting, reported the situation, and had a powerful prayer meeting.

11. We probably would have prayed for protection, but what did they pray for?

    *Acts 4:29–31—And now, Lord, behold their threatenings: and **grant unto [Your] servants, that with all boldness they may speak [Your] word**. . . . And when they had prayed, **the place was shaken** where they were assembled together; and **they were all filled with the Holy Ghost**, and they [spoke] the word of God with boldness.*

Notice the result of their prayers. God often used miraculous events in those early days to demonstrate His pleasure, and in some cases displeasure, with His people. Though we may not experience God shaking the ground when we pray, we can expect God to continue to give boldness to those who look to Him for it. Years later the apostle Paul was still asking for that same boldness.

12. What words in these prayer requests indicate the importance of grace and boldness in evangelism?

    *Ephesians 6:18–20—Praying always with all prayer and supplication in the Spirit, and watching thereunto with all perseverance and supplication for all saints; and for me, that **utterance may be given unto me**, that I may **open my mouth boldly**, to make known the mystery of the gospel, for which I am an ambassador in bonds: that therein **I may speak boldly, as I ought to speak**.*

    _____

    *Colossians 4:3–6—Withal praying also for us, that God would open unto us **a door of utterance**, to speak the mystery of Christ, for which I am also in bonds: that I may **make it manifest, as I ought to speak**. Walk in wisdom toward them that are without, redeeming the time. **Let your speech be always with grace**, seasoned with salt, that [you] may know how [you] ought to answer every man.*

    _____

THE POWER

13. What picture did Jesus use to show the abundant supply of power available to His servants?

    *John 7:38–39—He that [believes] on me, as the scripture [has] said, **out of his belly shall flow rivers of living water**. (But **this [spoke] he of the Spirit**, which they that believe on him should receive . . .)*

    _____

14. What did Jesus tell His disciples to do that demonstrated the necessity of the Holy Spirit's power in soulwinning?

    *Luke 24:49—And, behold, I send the promise of my Father upon you: but **tarry** . . . in the city of Jerusalem, **until [you] be endued with power from on high**.*

    _____

The New Testament is filled with examples of the Holy Spirit's power displayed in evangelism. One such story is found in Acts 18, when Paul first arrived in the city of Corinth. He had faced persecution from the unbelieving religious leaders in many of the cities he had visited, and he faced it again in Corinth. God spoke to him in a dream one night to give him courage to continue preaching.

    *Acts 18:9–10—Then [spoke] the Lord to Paul in the night by a vision, **Be not afraid, but speak**, and hold not [your] peace: for I am with [you], and no man shall set on [you] to hurt [you]: for **I have much people in this city**.*

In the passage below Paul recounts those early days in a letter to the Corinthians.

15. Did Paul depend on his own oratory skills to convince men to turn to Jesus?

    *1 Corinthians 2:1–5—And I, brethren, when I came to you, **came not with excellency of speech** or of wisdom, declaring unto you the testimony of God. For I determined not to know any thing among you, save Jesus Christ, and him crucified. And I was with you in weakness, and in fear, and in much trembling. And my speech and my preaching was not with enticing words of man's wisdom, but in demonstration of the Spirit and of power: that your faith should not stand in the wisdom of men, but in the power of God.*

    _____

What was his focus?

For **I determined not to know any thing among you, save Jesus Christ, and him crucified.**

How did Paul characterize his abilities and emotions?

And I was with you in **weakness**, and in **fear**, and in **much trembling**.

What characterized his preaching?

And my speech and my preaching was not with enticing words of man's wisdom, but in **demonstration of the Spirit and of power.**

Why doesn't God remove our own weaknesses and fears when He gives us His power?

That **your faith should** not **stand** in the wisdom of men, but **in the power of God**.

Second Corinthians 2:14–7:6 is an unusually transparent glimpse into the heart of Paul and demonstrates these wonderful characteristics of God's power on display through his frail human life. I love the use of the word *manifest* throughout this passage. It powerfully captures the Christ-life principle. Christ's life was evidenced in Paul's life, though he still felt weak and even afraid.

16. Can you describe the fragrance of Christ in this familiar passage?

*2 Corinthians 2:14–16—Now thanks be unto God, which always [causes] us to triumph in Christ, and [makes] manifest the savour [fragrances] of his knowledge by us in every place. For **we are unto God a sweet savour of Christ, in them that are saved, and in them that perish**: to the one we are the savour of death unto death; and to the other the savour of life unto life. And who is sufficient for these things? For we are not as many, which corrupt the word of God: but as of sincerity, but as of God, in the sight of God speak we in Christ.*

In what two ways is the invisible, powerful, invasive aura of Christ in the Spirit-filled Christian's life perceived?

*To the one we are **the savour of death unto death**; and to the other **the savour of life unto life**. And who is sufficient for these things?*

We do not determine how people perceive the aura of Christ in our lives. We determine only that we are filled with His fragrance. Some people will sense the sweet fragrance of Christ in our lives as fresh and as attractive as the sweet smell of springtime. Others will sense the same fragrance but will hate it as much as they despise the smell of death. God will use this fragrance to give us an invisible powerful attractiveness to some, but the same invisible "aura" will be repulsive to others. Paul says that attraction or repugnancy will result in life to some and death to the others. This

119

must have been what Jim Elliott had in mind when he said, "Father, make me a crisis man. Bring those I contact to decision. Let me not be a milepost on a single road: make me a fork, that men must turn one way or the other on facing Christ in me."

17. What is necessary before we can see the fragrance of Christ result in life to some?

For we are not as many, which corrupt the word of God: but as of sincerity, but as of God, in the sight of God **speak we in Christ**.

_____

Some in Paul's day tried to "corrupt" the Word of God by "peddling" Christ. A peddler would put the best apples on top of his basket and leave the less desirable ones hidden underneath. Paul was determined to speak the truth simply about Jesus in the power of God and let the Word speak for itself.

Spirit empowered believers must be bold and proclaim the good news of the gospel.

In 2 Corinthians 4 Paul continued his discussion about the power of the gospel by emphasizing the urgency of not letting the good news of Jesus be hidden.

18. Who will suffer if we hide our gospel witness?

2 Corinthians 4:3–7—But **if our gospel be hid, it is hid to them that are lost**: *in whom the god of this world [has] blinded the minds of them which believe not, lest the light of the glorious gospel of Christ, who is the image of God, should shine unto them. For we preach not ourselves, but Christ Jesus the Lord; and ourselves your servants for Jesus' sake. For God, who commanded the light to shine out of darkness, [has] shined in our hearts, to give the light of the knowledge of the glory of God in the face of Jesus Christ. But we have this treasure in earthen vessels, that the excellency of the power may be of God, and not of us.*

_____

Who is the God of this world?

_____

How do we combat his evil intent?

For we **preach** *not ourselves, but* **Christ Jesus the Lord**; *and ourselves your servants for Jesus' sake. For God, who commanded the light to shine out of darkness, [has] shined in our hearts, to* **give the light** *of the knowledge of the glory of God in the face of Jesus Christ.*

_____

Do you have what it takes to let people see the light of the glorious gospel of Christ?

But **we have this treasure in earthen vessels**, *that* **the excellency of the power** *may be of God, and not of us.*

_____

19. How did your life change when Christ saved you?

   *2 Corinthians 5:17–20—Therefore **if any man be in Christ, he is a new creature**: old things are passed away; behold, **all things are become new**. And all things are of God, who [has] reconciled us to himself by Jesus Christ, and [has] given to us the ministry of reconciliation; To wit, that God was in Christ, reconciling the world unto himself, not imputing their trespasses unto them; and [has] committed unto us the word of reconciliation. Now then we are ambassadors for Christ, as though God did beseech you by us: we pray you in Christ's stead, be . . . reconciled to God.*

   _____

20. What ministry did God give you when He reconciled you to Himself through Jesus' exchange?

   *And all things are of God, who [has] reconciled us to himself by Jesus Christ, and [has] given to us **the ministry of reconciliation**; to wit, that God was in Christ, reconciling the world unto himself, not imputing their trespasses unto them; and [has] committed unto us **the word [message] of reconciliation**.*

   _____

   What human position does God use to help us see our role in dealing with the lost world?

   Now then we are ambassadors for Christ, *as though God did beseech you by us: we pray you **in Christ's stead**, be . . . reconciled to God.*

   _____

An ambassador is sent as an official representative to a foreign country. Notice the urgency and passion with which Paul exercised his role as Christ's ambassador. As we are filled by His Holy Spirit, God wants us to display the life of Christ in our actions and even in our inner passions. The next verse is one of the clearest expressions in the Bible of the exchange Christ offers the world.

   2 Corinthians 5:21—For he [has] made him to be sin for us, who knew no sin; that we might be made the righteousness of God in him.

21. Will you answer God's call to be His ambassador and tell those around you about this wonderful exchange?

   _____

THE NEED FOR A GOSPEL WITNESS

22. Who is the only way of salvation?

   *John 14:6—Jesus [said] unto him, I am the way, the truth, and the life: **no man [comes] unto the Father, but by me**.*

   *Acts 4:12—Neither is there salvation in any other: for **there is none other name** under heaven given among men, **whereby we must be saved**.*

   _____

THE COURAGE FOR A GOSPEL WITNESS

23. What promise was given the disciples that would enable them to take the gospel to the entire world?

    *Acts 1:8—But [you] shall receive **power**, after that the Holy Ghost is come upon you: and [you] shall be witnesses unto me both in Jerusalem, and in all Judaea, and in Samaria, and unto the uttermost part of the earth.*

    _____

24. What does the Holy Spirit provide to replace our fears?

    *2 Timothy 1:7—For God [has] not given us the spirit of fear; but of **power**, and of **love**, and of a **sound mind**.*

    a.

    _____

    b.

    _____

    c.

    _____

God knows our tendency to fear. Remember that His victory does not remove our fleshly weaknesses, but it does overcome them with a stronger law. As a Spirit-filled Christian the power and love of God is flowing through your heart. When you choose to follow the prompting of the Holy Spirit to speak in the power of Christ, He energizes your mind with all that you have learned about Christ and uses you to effectively dispense Himself to the hearer.

THE MOTIVE FOR THE GOSPEL WITNESS

25. Who does God want to save?

    *2 Peter 3:9—The Lord is not slack concerning his promise, as some men count slackness; but is longsuffering to us-ward, **not willing that any should perish, but that all should come to repentance**.*

    *1 Timothy 2:3–4—God our Saviour; **who will have all men to be saved**, and to come unto the knowledge of the truth.*

    *Revelation 22:17—And the Spirit and the bride [the church] say, Come. And let him that [hears] say, Come. And let him that is athirst come. And **whosoever will**, let him take the water of life freely.*

    _____

26. What does God want us to expect when we give people the gospel?

    *John 4:35—Say not . . . There are yet four months, and then [comes] harvest? behold, I say unto you, Lift up your eyes, and look on the fields; for **they are white already to harvest**.*

    _____

27. What does the Bible say about a person who wins others to Christ?

*Proverbs 11:30—The fruit of the righteous is a tree of life; and **he that [wins] souls is wise**.*

THE METHOD FOR A GOSPEL WITNESS

28. What is the power of God unto salvation?

*Romans 1:14–16—I am debtor both to the Greeks, and to the Barbarians; both to the wise, and to the unwise. So, as much as in me is, I am ready to preach the gospel to you that are at Rome also. For I am not ashamed of **the gospel of Christ**: for it is **the power of God unto salvation** to every one that [believes]; to the Jew first, and also to the Greek.*

---

29. What does the Holy Spirit do when we tell men about sin, judgment, and the righteousness Jesus offers us in His exchange?

*John 16:8—And when he [the Holy Spirit] is come, **he will reprove [convince] the world of sin, and of righteousness, and of judgment**.*

---

30. What three activities were the responsibilities of the servants in this parable?

*Matthew 22:9–10—**Go** . . . therefore into the highways, and as many as [you] shall **find**, **bid** [invite] to the marriage. So those servants **went** out into the highways, and **gathered** together all as many as they **found**, both bad and good: and the wedding was furnished with guests.*

God has not called us to be salesmen with the responsibility to convince men to "buy" our **religion**. We are ambassadors introducing men to Christ and urgently inviting them to accept His exchange. The gospel itself is powerful. When we give the clear gospel message, the Holy Spirit promises to do the convincing for us. Our only responsibility is to **go, find** people who will listen, and **invite** them to come to see Jesus for themselves. When they see Him like you see Him, they will want the same **relationship** with Him you have.

31. In Mark 4:1–20 Christ compared giving out the Word of God to sowing seed. What principles of sowing are found in the following passages?

*Psalm 126:5–6—They that **sow in tears** shall **reap in joy**. He that [goes] forth and [weeps], bearing precious seed, shall **doubtless come again with rejoicing, bringing his sheaves with him**.*

---

*2 Corinthians 9:6—But this I say, He which [sows] **sparingly** shall **reap** also **sparingly**; and he which [sows] **bountifully** shall reap also **bountifully**.*

---

*Galatians 6:9—And let us not be weary in well doing: for in due season **we shall reap, if we faint not**.*

_____

God wants us to approach soulwinning with the expectation of reaping a ready harvest. If we don't find a harvest, our response is to plant the seed or water where someone else has already planted. Our job is not to produce the fruit; God gives the increase. Our job is to faithfully work in God's fields, constantly looking for ripe fruit to reap.

THE CLEAR PRESENTATION OF THE GOSPEL

32. What experience did Paul use to witness to others? Look up Acts 22:1–15 in your Bible and read it to find the answer.

_____

33. In order to make your testimony of salvation clear, make sure it includes these three points.

    Matthew 18:11—For the Son of man is come to save that which was lost.

    I knew I was _____.

    *John 1:12—But as many as **received him [Jesus]**, to them gave he power to become the sons of God, even to them that believe on his name.*

    I received _____.

    *2 Corinthians 5:17—Therefore if any man be in Christ, **he is a new creature**: old things are passed away; behold, **all things are become new**.*

    My life is _____.

Using this outline write your testimony in the space provided at the end of this lesson. Paul's verbal testimony is recorded three times in the book of Acts. Each time it is a compelling story. Don't just record the facts but tell the compelling story of Christ in your life.

34. Try to share your salvation testimony with at least one other person before the next class. Describe the results below.

_____

_____

_____

_____

God has revealed Himself to mankind in the Bible so that we can know Him. If you want someone to form a close relationship with Christ, you will have to introduce Him so that they can get to know Him for themselves. You can begin by showing them four of His basic characteristics.

God is holy and cannot tolerate our sin.

Romans 3:23—For all have sinned, and come short of the glory of God.

God is just and cannot overlook our sin.

Romans 6:23—The wages of sin is death.

God is loving and has reached out to us. He has provided a way for us to be close to Him that satisfies His holy and just nature.

1 Peter 3:18—For Christ also [has] once suffered for sins, the just for the unjust, that he might bring us to God.

God is gracious and offers salvation as a gift.

John 1:12—But as many as received him, to them gave he power to become the sons of God, even to them that believe on his name.

Do you want to witness more effectively for Christ? _____ Your Bible study leader will tell you about an exciting opportunity for you to learn to be a better soulwinner!

First Samuel records the story of Hannah. She was heartbroken because she couldn't have children. She was so burdened about her situation that she went to the temple and begged the Lord for a son. Hannah's prayer had three ingredients.

- Hannah knew **something was wrong**.

- Hannah knew **normal activities would not solve** the problem.

- **Hannah appealed** to God's throne of grace to do what only God can do.

In 1853 Andrew Bonar wrote, "God likes to see His people shut up to this—that there is no hope but in prayer. Herein lies the church's power against the world." Would you be willing to pray "the Hannah prayer" that God would give you a soul to lead to Christ?

The acrostic "ASK FOR IT" reminds us How to Be a Determined Disciple-Maker

Matthew 7:7—Ask, and it shall be given you; seek, and [you] shall find; knock, and it shall be opened unto you.

ASK!

SEEK!

KNOCK!

Matthew 7:8—For every one that [asks receives]; and he that [seeks finds]; and to him that [knocks] it shall be opened.

FIND!
OPEN!
RECEIVE!

Matthew 22:9–10—Go . . . therefore into the highways, and as many as [you] shall find, bid to the marriage. So those servants went out into the highways, and gathered together all as many as they found, both bad and good: and the wedding was furnished with guests.

INVITE!
TRAIN!

Andrew Murray wrote, "It has not entered into the heart of man to conceive what God will do for His child who gives himself to believe that his prayer will be heard!"

APPLICATION

James 1:22–25 promises God's special blessing on those who take action on what His Word teaches. Paul wrote about one family who approached ministry in a very zealous way.

*1 Corinthians 16:15—[You] know the house of Stephanas, that it is the first-fruits of Achaia, and that **they have addicted themselves to the ministry** of the saints.*

How do you think God wants you to approach ministry? Are you willing to be used of Him as He draws men to Himself through soulwinning? Write your resolve in a prayer.

_____

_____

_____

_____

_____

_____

God's perfect plan for you is to serve Him in your local church. To what ministries do you sense He is leading you?

_____

_____

_____

_____

_____

_____

ASSIGNMENTS

Bible Reading: Romans 1–7

Scripture Memory:

John 15:16—[You] have not chosen me, but I have chosen you, and ordained you, that [you] should go and bring forth fruit, and that your fruit should remain: that whatsoever [you] shall ask of the Father in my name, he may give it you.

(This verse is part of *The Exchange Scripture* Memory System.)

Practical Assignment: Ask your Bible study leader to help you find a ministry where you can begin to serve the King.

APPENDIX

INTERESTING FACTS

- God used 40 different men over a period of 1,500 years

- (about 1400 b.c. to a.d. 90) in writing the Bible (II Peter 1:20-21).

- Books of Old Testament—39

- Books of New Testament—27

- Total number of books—66

- Chapters in the Old Testament—929

- Chapters in the New Testament—260

- Total number of chapters—1,189

- Esther 8:9 is the longest verse.

- John 11:35 is the shortest verse.

- Paul wrote more books than any other New Testament writer.

- Luke wrote more words than any other New Testament writer (Luke and Acts).

- Job is probably the oldest book in the Bible.

- III John is the shortest book in the Greek New Testament.

- James and Jude were both the half brothers of Christ.

BOOKS OF THE BIBLE

THE NEW IS IN THE OLD CONCEALED

OLD TESTAMENT (39 BOOKS)
Looks forward to Christ's sacrifice on the cross

THE OLD IS IN THE NEW REVEALED

NEW TESTAMENT (27 BOOKS)
Based on the work of Christ finished on the cross

HISTORY 17 books **Law**	POETRY 5 books	PROPHECY 17 books		HISTORY 5 books **Gospels**	TEACHING 21 books	PROPHECY 1 book
1 Genesis	1 Job	Major Prophets		1 Matthew	Paul's Letters	Revelation
2 Exodus	2 Psalms	1 Isaiah		2 Mark	1 Romans	
3 Leviticus	3 Proverbs	2 Jeremiah		3 Luke	2 I Corinthians	
4 Numbers	4 Ecclesiastes	3 Lamentations		4 John	3 II Corinthians	
5 Deuteronomy	5 Song of	4 Ezekiel		5 Acts	4 Galatians	
	Solomon	5 Daniel			5 Ephesians	
History and Government		**Minor Prophets**			6 Philippians	
					7 Colossians	
1 Joshua		1 Hosea			8 I Thessalonians	
2 Judges		2 Joel			9 II Thessalonians	
3 Ruth		3 Amos			10 I Timothy	
4 I Samuel		4 Obadiah			11 II Timothy	
5 II Samuel		5 Jonah			12 Titus	
6 I Kings		6 Micah			13 Philemon	
7 II Kings		7 Nahum				
8 I Chronicles		8 Habakkuk			**General Letters**	
9 II Chronicles		9 Zephaniah			1 Hebrews	
10 Ezra		10 Haggai			2 James	
11 Nehemiah		11 Zechariah			3 I Peter	
12 Esther		12 Malachi			4 II Peter	
					5 I John	
					6 II John	
					7 III John	
					8 Jude	

(vertical divider text: ABOUT 400 YEARS BETWEEN TESTAMENTS)

Special thanks to John Van Gelderen for providing this information.

BOOK	CHAPTERS (mark when read)																					
Matthew	1	2	3	4	5	6	7	8	9	10	11	12	13	14	15	16	17	18	19	20	21	22
	23	24	25	26	27	28																
Mark	1	2	3	4	5	6	7	8	9	10	11	12	13	14	15	16						
Luke	1	2	3	4	5	6	7	8	9	10	11	12	13	14	15	16	17	18	19	20	21	22
	23	24																				
John	1	2	3	4	5	6	7	8	9	10	11	12	13	14	15	16	17	18	19	20	21	
Acts	1	2	3	4	5	6	7	8	9	10	11	12	13	14	15	16	17	18	19	20	21	22
	23	24	25	26	27	28																
Romans	1	2	3	4	5	6	7	8	9	10	11	12	13	14	15	16						
I Corinthians	1	2	3	4	5	6	7	8	9	10	11	12	13	14	15	16						
II Corinthians	1	2	3	4	5	6	7	8	9	10	11	12	13									
Galatians	1	2	3	4	5	6																
Ephesians	1	2	3	4	5	6																
Philippians	1	2	3	4																		
Colossians	1	2	3	4																		
I Thessalonians	1	2	3	4	5																	
II Thessalonians	1	2	3																			
I Timothy	1	2	3	4	5	6																
II Timothy	1	2	3	4																		
Titus	1	2	3																			
Philemon	1																					
Hebrews	1	2	3	4	5	6	7	8	9	10	11	12	13									
James	1	2	3	4	5																	
I Peter	1	2	3	4	5																	
II Peter	1	2	3																			
I John	1	2	3	4	5																	
II John	1																					
III John	1																					
Jude	1																					
Revelation	1	2	3	4	5	6	7	8	9	10	11	12	13	14	15	16	17	18	19	20	21	22